LEADERSHIP

A PRACTICAL GUIDE

ALISON & DAVID PRICE

Published in the UK and USA
in 2013 by Icon Books Ltd,
Omnibus Business Centre,
39–41 North Road,
London N7 9DP
email: info@iconbooks.net
www.iconbooks.net

Distributed in Australia and
New Zealand
by Allen & Unwin Pty Ltd,
PO Box 8500,
83 Alexander Street,
Crows Nest,
NSW 2065

Sold in the UK, Europe and Asia
by Faber & Faber Ltd,
Bloomsbury House,
74–77 Great Russell Street,
London WC1B 3DA
or their agents

Distributed in Canada
by Penguin Books Canada,
90 Eglinton Avenue East,
Suite 700, Toronto,
Ontario M4P 2Y3

Distributed in South Africa
by Book Promotions,
Office B4, The District,
41 Sir Lowry Road,
Woodstock 7925

Distributed to the trade in the USA
by Consortium Book Sales
and Distribution,
The Keg House,
34 Thirteenth Avenue NE, Suite 101,
Minneapolis, MN 55413-1007

ISBN: 978-184831-511-2

Typeset in Avenir by Marie Doherty

Printed and bound in the UK by Clays Ltd, St Ives plc

About the authors

Alison Price is a Chartered Occupational Psychologist who has coached senior leaders in prestigious organizations and has designed leadership training programmes attended by thousands of people.

In 2009, Alison was a semi-finalist in 'Britain's Next Top Coach'. Alison also lectures on a master's-level course in Business Psychology at a London University. She offers her services through her company The Success Agents.

David Price is a senior manager and has led award-winning teams within prestigious financial services organizations. David has qualifications in management and coaching and is a qualified Member of the Chartered Management Institute.

Further information about the authors and resources on leadership can be found at the following website:

www.leadership-handbook.com

Authors' note

This book contains frequently used research and methods. Where we know the source we have been sure to reference it, but our apologies here to the originators of any material if we have overlooked them.

Dedication

This book is dedicated to Alison's sister, Jacqueline Hardt – great leaders build confidence and esteem in their people, while simultaneously inspiring them and challenging them to raise the bar and perform at their very best. Your ability to demonstrate these leadership skills was invaluable to us when writing this book, so thank you.

Contents

Introduction

In a bid to embrace the power of new technology, we placed the following comment on a social networking site:

> Google gives employees a free massage on their birthday. Does anyone have any examples like this (your own or others) of how leaders can create an environment at work that motivates their people?

We normally get a great response to requests like this; however, on this occasion we only received two replies:

1. 'I could give you plenty of examples of how we're demotivated.'

2. 'Yes me too.'

Imagine these people were part of your organization. Would it surprise you to hear comments like this?

Let's not beat about the bush, leadership can be tough. New leaders are often required to step out of the shadow of a previous leader, perhaps establishing themselves as the person in charge when previously they were a peer. If you're new to an organization, you have to adapt to its culture, then, just as you've got used to the way things are done, everything changes and you need to be ready to lead yourself and others into unchartered and hostile territory. Sometimes your work is underpinned by crippling personal doubt: *'Can I do this?'*, *'Is it worth it?'* And even *after* you've succeeded, when things hit a rough patch, people start questioning whether it's time for you to leave. From the point where you step up to the point that you bow out, you're in the spotlight (and the firing line) with people looking to you to keep them motivated and constantly deliver results.

But it's by no means all doom and gloom. There are many examples of great leaders who achieved brilliant things against all odds, and you'll find this book packed with their real-life ideas, strategies and tried and tested winning solutions to challenges that you face. So whether you're starting from scratch as a new leader, an existing leader who needs to raise their game, or just want to aim higher and do what the best leaders do, you'll be inspired both by what they have achieved and what you have the potential to achieve.

The difference between leadership and management

People often ask how leadership and management differ. One of the best ways to describe this is using Stephen Covey's jungle analogy. The worker on the ground is busy cutting down trees and undergrowth. The manager supports the worker, keeping him on task and on track. The leader, however, is the person who climbs the tallest tree, surveys the area and works out if they are heading in the right direction. The leader points the way for the others to follow.

Picture yourself at the top of that tree. It is your job to understand the big picture environment – where are the 'thunderstorms' that can impact your operations? The leader should also look down and keep in touch with how operations are progressing on the ground. For example, can you see any issues across teams which are consistently hindering operations? Is the delivery of the overall operation progressing at the expected pace and to the right standard? The leader also needs to ask, is this still the right jungle to cut down?

Where leaders spot new luscious jungles to conquer, they need to be confident that their vision for the future is viable and secure the resources needed to plan and execute it. Since they can't do all the work themselves, they need to inspire other people to believe in their goals and motivate them to channel their energy towards it, sometimes operating from outside of their comfort zone in challenging situations.

Finally, strong leaders come down from their tree and spend time on the ground, among their people. They seek to understand what it's really like down in the jungle, set an example, recognize effort and achievement and inspire high performance during good times and bad.

You'll find all of this – plus more – covered in this book.

The difference that makes the difference!

When we first began working in the leadership arena we studied many effective leaders, hoping to identify, for each person, the *one thing* that was critical to their success. However, we quickly discovered that there was never a *single* factor that made the difference. In contrast, it was the sum of many individual parts that came together to create the whole.

So we then asked the question, 'Well, what is the magic combination of factors that drives leadership success?' We were attempting to create a helpful recipe – so that if you put the ingredients together, you could generate a great outcome. However, yet again, we discovered there is *no definitive set of factors* that makes leaders brilliant.

Instead, through our research and our work in developing successful leaders, we have come to realize that leadership is like using an artist's palette. The colours represent the strengths that support leaders to excel, such as great oratory skills, calmness under pressure and the ability to make effective decisions. But no two leaders will ever paint the exact same picture. No leader uses the same combination of colours as another leader. And, just like art, although some pieces are clearly better-loved than others, there is rarely unanimous agreement of brilliance. Even the most popular leaders can have their critics.

You can think of this book like an artist's painting box. We've covered the key colours that make leaders effective, for you to explore and practise applying with your brushstrokes. You will use some colours more than others and you may not use some at all. You can experiment by consciously applying these leadership skill 'colours' as you attempt to create your own masterpiece.

You will notice that we refer to the same leaders multiple times throughout the book. Since there was never one thing that made a leader brilliant, it's useful to look at the multiple aspects that helped them to succeed. Imagine that we are painting a picture, and each time we refer to a leader again, we are adding a new colour to the canvas, creating a richer picture overall.

Finally, as you review the case studies of real-life leadership which depict a great use of a specific skill, we recommend that you focus on learning about the *particular area* which is the subject matter of the chapter. It's very easy to become distracted by other elements of a person's leadership – *'They may have been good at x, but they were useless at y!'* And we agree with you, but that doesn't mean you can't learn a lot from specific things that leaders *were* good at.

The A–Z of leadership

Finally, each of the chapters in this book links to a different letter of the alphabet. In our home country, the United Kingdom, an A–Z is a map book – something that helps people to have smooth journeys and to get back on track when things go wrong. We very much hope that our A–Z is a useful guide to you as you continue on your own leadership journey.

Alison & David Price

A: Aspiration

*Never tell me the sky's the limit when there are
footprints on the moon.*
– Author unknown

In the introduction, we explained that there is no single definitive set of factors common to all great leaders. There was, however, one common theme that did crop up time and time again – leaders aspire to achieve goals. This chapter therefore explores the fuel that ignites their vision and how they transform a compelling idea into a clear guiding focus for yourself and others to follow.

Dark times ignite change

As the pastor Charles Swindoll once said: 'We are all faced with a series of great opportunities brilliantly disguised as impossible situations.' For a young, unassuming Indian lawyer named Mohandas Gandhi, this took the form of a train journey in 1893, from the British Colony Natal in South Africa to Pretoria. Although Gandhi originally travelled to South Africa for work, this train journey would change the course of his own life and many others worldwide.

Gandhi held a ticket for first class; however, despite being impeccably dressed in a suit and causing no trouble whatsoever, a white passenger complained about his presence – Indians were not allowed in first class. Gandhi was therefore humiliatingly ordered to move to third class. When he refused to move, he was thrown off the train and spent the night shivering at the station. Throughout the long, cold night, he pondered the sobering alternative: 'Should I go back to India or should I stay in South Africa and fight for my rights?'

Gandhi soon uncovered far more injustice in South Africa – Indians could only build homes in areas set apart for them. They were forbidden from going out at night without a permit and Gandhi was even forcibly removed from walking on a footpath. Gandhi had spotted a chance to improve a very negative situation and he felt fired up to pursue it. The seeds of his vision had been laid.

Spot an enticing opportunity

While some visions, like Gandhi's, are sparked by dark times, others are born out of situations that are fundamentally OK but where far-sighted people see that there is an exciting opportunity to be grasped. For example, in the late 1970s, Sir Richard Branson and his partner Joan were on holiday in the British Virgin Islands and were trying to catch a plane to Puerto Rico when their flight was cancelled. The airport terminal was full of stranded passengers, so Branson made a few phone calls and agreed to charter a plane for $2,000. He then divided the price by the remaining number of passengers, borrowed a blackboard and wrote: 'VIRGIN AIRWAYS: $39 for a single flight to Puerto Rico'. Bookings poured in and Branson was so inspired by his achievement that, on his return home, he called the air-craft manufacturer Boeing to ask how much it would cost to lease a second-hand plane for a year. A new business opportunity had been spotted and the first step towards launching his airline had been taken.

Great things are born from great opportunity – either to rectify a negative situation or opti-mize a positive one.

Pick a compelling opportunity in your own life where you can be a leader who inspires positive change. Draw a picture to represent what you want to achieve in future. You can work on creating this vision throughout the book.

X marks the spot

You can think of a vision as a treasure map – something that identifies where you aspire to be in the future. People (including the leader!) should be able to clearly describe the future state that they are heading towards. For example, prior to the launch of his airline business, Branson described his vision for Virgin Atlantic – to create a 'high quality, enjoyable and value for money airline'. Through this short description of his vision you can easily understand Branson's business idea. Clear visions are helpful because they create a common understanding of what needs to be achieved, and they enable everyone to channel their efforts in the same direction.

Visions often evolve over time – using our treasure map analogy you can reach a location where treasure is buried and then move on towards another location in search of further bounty. For example, Gandhi's early vision was to fight against Indian discrimination in Natal, South Africa. However, many years later, his focus shifted towards attaining 'Home rule for India', therefore aiming to free the nation from the rule of the British Empire.

Even when your vision is evolving, you still need to ensure that you have a single core focus. While you can efficiently work towards reaching one specific place, when you are simultaneously aiming for multiple crosses on a map, you can experience a sense of chaos.

This situation was faced by Steve Jobs in 1997, on his return to the helm of the computer company Apple. He found that while employees were working hard, they were channelling their efforts in numerous disordered directions. This meant they were struggling to produce anything and what they were creating was often of a poor standard. As a result, profits were plummeting and the company was close to becoming bankrupt.

Three elements that support a good vision

Specificity: Linking back to our treasure map analogy, the treasure will be much easier to find if you know precisely the spot where you are aiming for. The same goes for visions. Branson's vision to launch a 'high quality, enjoyable and value for money airline' and Gandhi's vision to achieve

'Home rule for India' are both specific, tangible and easy to understand. As was NASA's vision statement regarding their goal to put man on the moon: 'Perform a manned lunar landing and return.'

Succinctness: Being succinct helps to achieve clarity, especially if what you are trying to explain is actually quite complex. For example, when striving to obtain funding to launch Google, Sergey Brin and Larry Page needed to describe the vision for their business and were able to do this in one sentence: 'Google provides access to the world's information in one click.' A good rule of thumb is that a vision should be communicable in ten words or less.

Emotional connection: Visions should excite and inspire the listener, and that means that a vision needs to be all about them and *not* all about you. Let's take Branson's 1984 vision for Virgin Atlantic and hypothetically reword it to make it all about him: 'Our vision is to make money by providing a new airline.' This clearly does not have the same impact! In contrast, back in 1984, the prospect of travelling on a plane that would revolutionize the industry – with entertainment, panache and tasty food – provided at a lower cost than traditional air travel, was a different and enticing prospect.

Aim to summarize your goal into a vision statement. Make sure that this statement:

• Is ten words or less

10

- Specifically states what you are aiming to achieve

- Creates an emotional connection with the listener.

The difference between a vision and a mission

People often get confused between the concepts of a 'vision' and a 'mission', partly because there are many conflicting definitions of what visions and missions are. Put most simply:

- A vision is where you aspire to be in the future.

- Your mission is what you aspire to do, at your best, every day – the philosophy being that if you excel at your mission, you will achieve your vision.

If the vision is symbolized by a cross on a map, the metaphor for a mission is footprints in the sand – in other words the journey towards a vision. Your mission summarizes your purpose, in other words what you are there to do on a day-to-day basis.

To explore this further, let's take Gandhi's *vision* to achieve 'Home rule for India'. Gandhi dreamed that in the future India would no longer be ruled by the British Empire.

His *mission* was 'non-violent resistance'. On a day-to-day basis, the Indian people needed to peacefully resist British rule, for example by marching in protest, holding rallies and by stimulating mass boycotts of British goods such as clothing and salt. Gandhi's hope was that, over time, this type of aggravating behaviour would become so problematic to the British government in India, that it would give way and allow India to become an independent nation. In other words the mission would lead to the achievement of the vision.

But do I really need this vision and mission stuff?

We have come across leaders who believe that visions and missions are just fancy words on a page that are not really needed. This shows that they have totally missed the point of these powerful concepts.

A vision summarizes what you are aspiring to achieve – it is at the heart of where you are headed and succinctly describes what success will look like. Your priority should not be 'wordsmithing'; instead you must ensure that the essence of the vision itself is right and that you truly understand what future state you aspire to achieve. If you can't describe this, how can you expect others to follow you there? Also ask yourself whether you are excited by the prospect of achieving your vision – if you aren't, it's unlikely that other people will be either.

Your vision and mission should help to drive everyday decisions. For example, if you want to achieve 'Home rule for India' through *non-violent resistance*, would your mission be to kill someone who sought to take away your rights? Probably not.

The power of a leader with a vision can be seen through Branson and Gandhi's legacy. Today Virgin Atlantic flies to over 30 destinations worldwide and carries around 5 million passengers each year. Under Gandhi's leadership India achieved independence to govern themselves in 1947.

 Great things are born from great opportunity – either to rectify a negative situation or optimize a positive one. When a leader spots such a chance and creates a compelling vision, amazing things can be achieved.

B: Backing

If you can dream it, you can do it.
– Walt Disney

The world is full of people with grand visions that have the potential to change lives. Yet many of these remain nothing more than good ideas. Convincing other people that you've come up with the best idea since sliced bread may seem easy until you ask them to invest money, time or energy! So how do leaders secure the backing required to evolve and sustain their grand ideas?

The vision
In the early 1940s Walt Disney sat on a park bench at a fairground and watched his young children riding on a merry-go-round. As he waited patiently for the ride to finish, he asked himself, 'Why isn't there a place where children and their parents can have fun together?' That moment marked the beginning of the dream to create the happiest place on earth – one with flying elephants and a magical fairy-tale castle – known affectionately today as 'Disneyland'.

Believe in your idea
If you don't believe in your idea, it's certain that no one else will, so leaders must have complete confidence in their vision and be able to defend it when it comes under

scrutiny. The path to realizing a vision is seldom easy. It takes courage and determination and you must live by the Japanese proverb, 'Fall down seven times, stand up eight.'

Disney faced an absolute barrage of criticism directed towards his big idea: 'You can't operate a theme park all year round', 'You won't make enough money', 'People don't care about the little details.' Despite numerous knock-backs from investors and acquaintances telling him he was 'completely nuts', Walt never gave up on his dream, so much so that he was prepared to mortgage his own house to help to pay for it.

As you will learn throughout this book, history's greatest leaders, such as Martin Luther King and Nelson Mandela, all had massive belief in their causes. This sense of certainty and purpose gave them the confidence they needed to keep going against all odds and to infect others with their enthusiasm, passion and determination.

Think about your vision now. On a scale of 1 to 10, how much are you passionately committed to what it is that you are trying to achieve (1 = not at all, 10 = completely and wholeheartedly)?

If you didn't answer 10, what are the things that you need to do to increase the score you gave? Write out a list.

Manage the downsides of risk

Even with the strongest belief in an idea, there is also a sobering message to be heard – if you are embarking on something new, you must manage the downsides of the risk.

Walt put himself (and his animation studio employees) in a very precarious position when financing Disneyland. If the theme park venture had failed, it would have brought the studio down with it, and his staff were very frightened about losing their jobs. Although ultimately things turned out fine for Walt, there are numerous other examples that do not have such fairy-tale endings.

Richard Branson gives sound advice to overcome this problem: 'Make bold moves but ensure there is a way out if something goes wrong.' This attitude was illustrated by his approach to transitioning from the music business to setting up an airline. When launching Virgin Atlantic, Branson leased a plane from Boeing that could be returned after twelve months if the business wasn't successful enough. Critically, this meant that if the venture failed, it would not bring down the rest of his business. Branson was quite clear that he did not want people in his music company to lose their jobs from a failed branch-out initiative.

By default of their position, leaders assume responsibilities for the livelihoods of other people and they need to take this responsibility seriously.

One of the most important phrases in my life is
protecting the downside.
– Richard Branson

Use your network to help you

Securing funding for Disneyland was no easy task. The final cost of building the California theme park was $17 million – in today's world, that figure would have been around ten times more. Inspiringly, this park bench vision was achieved by a man who earlier in his life had been virtually penniless.

Walt struggled to secure enough backing to build the park. He therefore called upon his brother, Roy, who was a commercial mastermind to help to come up with a solution.

Help isn't always something that us humans proactively seek. At school, we are proactively taught to *do things ourselves* – getting other people to do our work for us is bad and equates to cheating! There's also a certain sense of satisfaction to be gained from persevering and succeeding in solving a tough challenge ourselves – just think about how addictive a tough puzzle can be and how disappointing it feels when someone takes over and shows you the solution. However, astute leaders realize that they *should not try to do everything themselves*, and instead they should look to others to fill the gaps, providing a shortcut to success. They are aware of when they need support and they are not afraid to ask for it.

If you don't think that you know anyone who can help you, remember that the size of your network is far greater than the people you know personally. You may only know 500 people, but if those 500 people each know another 500 people, suddenly you have an enormous pool of opportunity.

For example, Richard Reed, Adam Balon and Jon Wright had failed to secure funding for their new smoothie business, despite numerous attempts. They were tens of thousands of pounds in debt, so, in a final act of desperation, they sent an email to everyone they could think of entitled 'Does anyone know anyone rich?' They got two replies, including one from a friend who had done work experience with a wealthy businessman called Maurice Pinto, who went on to make a £250,000 investment into their venture 'Innocent Drinks'.

 With regard to a goal that you want to achieve, write down where you could benefit from additional support. How can you take advantage of your network to help you with this?

Don't start from scratch – tap into your existing achievements

Moving from the animation business to opening a theme park was a pretty dramatic step, particularly when nothing like Disneyland had ever been created before. It can sometimes prove impossible for other people to make the leap of faith needed to buy into your idea. In the words of Disney, 'I could never convince the financiers that Disneyland was feasible, because dreams offer too little collateral.'

Starting from scratch equates to doing things the hard way – when struggling to achieve buy-in to an idea, ask yourself, 'What have I already achieved and how can this shortcut my route to success?'

Disney's strength lay in his track record in the cartoon business – he had been a successful animator for many years. Roy Disney therefore suggested asking television networks to invest in the theme park venture. In return for guaranteeing bank loans and for providing a small amount of direct funding, Disney could offer them a share of profits from the park, plus the opportunity to make a documentary programme about its construction. This was a potentially attractive offer, since Disney already had a strong cartoon fan base which the television network could capitalize on, before the financial returns from the park came to fruition.

After approaching a couple of different networks, the American Broadcast Company agreed to give Walt the backing he so desperately needed.

THINK ABOUT IT What existing assets or achievements do you already have that give you a foundation for your new initiative? How can you capitalize on these?

19

Formalize your agreement

The sweetest of deals can fail catastrophically when there is a breakdown in relationships between key partners. Key partners may involve financial backers, business owners or people that you integrate closely with.

Making formal agreements with partners, particularly if they are close acquaintances, may feel uncomfortable. People don't like asking difficult questions which could throw a potential deal off course, but failure to seek formalized agreements and details with key partners upfront can have massively detrimental effects in the longer term.

When launching a new initiative it is essential to ensure that the following has been achieved with all key partners:

- Ensure that you have a common and detailed understanding of the future course of action

- Ensure that you have a transparent and accurate view of resourcing requirements (e.g. time, money, personnel, etc.)

- Identify potential risks and how they can be mitigated

- Give explicit detail around any commitments made by either party, including any criteria that need to be achieved to activate a commitment

- Plan regular review meetings to monitor the above criteria.

It is recommended that the above are summarized in the format of a signed, written agreement, even if you already have a close or established relationship with your partner.

Identify any key partners involved in your idea. Ensure that you have covered the above checklist off with each key stakeholder and addressed any gaps.

The realization of a vision

Millions of people still visit Disneyland California each year. If you've ever had the privilege of looking up in awe at Walt's fairy-tale castle or catching a ride on one of his flying elephants, you'll know just how special Walt's vision was and how worthwhile his efforts to bring it to fruition were. When we visited Disneyland we were hugely inspired by a simple wooden bench with a small plaque that read, 'The actual park bench from the Griffith Park Merry-go-round in Los Angeles, where Walt Disney first dreamed of Disneyland.' Maybe it's time to take a stroll in the sun and pause for a while to reflect on a park bench – who knows what you will achieve as a result.

In order to make your vision a reality you will need belief in your idea, and you should con-sider how to protect as well as play to the strengths of the assets you have.

C: Compelling Communication

Speech is power: speech is to persuade, to convert,
to compel.
– Ralph Waldo Emerson

Once your inner circle of partners has bought into your idea, you may need to take your vision to a wider audience, which frequently takes the form of public speaking. You can think of public speaking as like baking: some people are naturally better at baking than others, but if you follow a recipe and keep practising, you are likely to get great results.

In this chapter we will take inspiration from two 'master chefs' of public speaking: John F. Kennedy, with his announcement at Rice University in 1962 to put 'Man on the moon'; and Martin Luther King, using his 'I have a dream' speech from 1963. Both dialogues are frequently listed in opinion polls of the greatest leadership speeches of all time. Interestingly, even though these two presentations are on very different subjects, they both cover six key themes. We will explore what these key themes are, and you can then use these to structure your own powerful leadership speeches.

If you have access to the internet, you might like to try to read and/or listen to both of the speeches referenced above before reading further.

---

1. Define where you and your audience are now

This serves both to introduce the platform for change and to mark the point that needs to be departed from.

- JFK stated that 'We meet in an hour of change and challenge, in a decade of hope and fear in an age of both knowledge and ignorance.' He referred both to America's (then) limited capacity for space travel, plus the more subtle message of the existence of an underlying power struggle with the Soviet Union.

- Martin Luther King described the existence of racial inequality, where black people were segregated from white people, experiencing poverty while other Americans were able to prosper.

2. Describe your goal

For the speech to be effective in stimulating change, the audience needs to understand the vision for change through a headline statement of what will be different or achieved in the future.

- JFK defined his goal to put man on the moon before the end of the decade. He passionately communicated that the space race was something America intended to win, while inferring that America would also remain as the leading superpower nation.

- Martin Luther King defined his goal of claiming the rights to life, liberty and the pursuit of happiness for all Americans, regardless of the colour of their skin.

3. Create a sense of urgency

Understanding the difference between a current and future state is largely irrelevant if people choose to take no action. Therefore a compelling argument that action is needed *now* is an important ingredient of a leadership speech about change.

- JFK asserted that the US was behind the Soviet Union when it came to manned space flight. However, he reiterated that the US would not stay behind – 'In this decade we shall make up and move ahead.'

- In one of the most powerful parts of Martin Luther King's speech, he repeatedly used the words 'Now is the time', creating a powerful call to action to rid America of racial injustice.

4. Reference the negative consequences of failing to achieve the vision

Having introduced the goal, it is then useful to expand upon the detrimental consequences that might occur, should the vision fail to be realized. This adds weight to the case for change by leading people to contemplate undesirable consequences.

- JFK referred to the possibility that space could become a hostile theatre of war, filled with weapons of mass destruction rather than instruments of knowledge and understanding.

- Martin Luther King described how black people could never be satisfied while experiencing police brutality or being denied access to basic human rights such as access to motels or the ability to vote.

5. Outline a positive view of the future should the vision be attempted/realized

It is motivating to also stress the benefits that will occur should the vision be realized. This works well if it follows a negative vision of the future, since the contrast from negative to positive exaggerates the advantages of change.

- JFK described the benefits that the quest to put man on the moon would bring, including the development of new tools and technologies and the creation of new companies and jobs.

- Martin Luther King described a new status quo where people would no longer be judged by their race but by the content of their character and where black children could play hand in hand with white children.

6. Describe the moment in time when the vision is realized

Both JFK and Martin Luther King ended their speeches by fast-forwarding in time, beyond all of the hard work that needed to be done, to the idealized moment where success is achieved. It acted as an inspirational ending to their speeches and also a reinforcement of what needed to be achieved.

- JFK described the path of a giant rocket, passing through the stresses and strains of space, reaching an unknown celestial body and returning safely to Earth. It was inspiring to visualize this journey and the moment of its magical landing – and it is even more thrilling to reflect upon this actually being achieved.

- Martin Luther King ended his speech with a beautiful vision of how freedom would ring in every village, hamlet, city and state. As he talked the audience could picture people celebrating their vastly deserved freedom. Although it is desperately sad that King was ultimately assassinated, the attention he brought to this cause changed the lives of millions of people.

Find examples of other inspirational speeches that outline a vision for the future, and look to see how they incorporated some or all of the above components.

From content to style

When cooking, using the right ingredients is one thing but having good technique is another important part of producing great food. We'll give you six bonus 'chef's tips' for delivering great speeches or presentations.

Tip one: Get people's attention early on

Many speeches begin slowly: 'My name is ...'; 'My previous experience includes ...'; 'I'd like to thank ...'; 'Welcome to today's hosts, guests, sponsors (aunties, next-door neighbours' dogs, etc., etc.)'. Yawn!

Since most people begin speeches with boring formalities, starting with the unexpected can make people sit up and pay attention.

In 2006, we attended a master class in training delivery and the facilitator abandoned the traditional opening format and launched straight into a story! The story powerfully made the point of why it was so important to attend the course and to learn related skills – much more effectively than simply being told. It also signalled that the course would be interesting and was worth paying attention to. We've used this trick many times since and have found that it creates a really good energy right from the start. We have found that you build credibility because you are delivering immediate results rather than waffling on about all of your academic and professional achievements.

If you do need to introduce yourself, for example to build credibility or offer votes of thanks, ensure that you don't lose people's attention before you have even begun. JFK chose to introduce his speech formally, offering votes of thanks, but this introduction was less than 30 seconds, so it did not detract from the remaining content.

If you are doing a formal introduction, it can be effective to create humour within the first minute of your speech. For example when J.K. Rowling addressed the Harvard graduating 'Class of 2008', she created a great roar of laughter during the opening section through thanking the university for inducing weeks of fear and nausea, which led her to lose weight! 'Now all I have to do is take deep breaths, squint at the red banners and convince myself that I am at the world's largest Gryffindor reunion!' The welcomes and vote of thanks were all completed within the space of 60 seconds and created several loud chuckles of laughter from the crowd. With such a positive opening, you know the rest of the speech is going to be worth listening to.

Tip two: Use repetitive language to stress important points

Martin Luther King powerfully used the phrase 'I have a dream' nine times, which built up an increasing sense of tension and emotion as he spoke. Perhaps by accident rather than design (due to the crowd cheering) JFK repeated the words 'We choose to go to the moon' three times, which put emphasis on the goal. Both of these phrases are among the most memorable parts of their respective speeches; as well as adding gravitas to your words, repetitive language increases the chance of the listener remembering the key message.

Tip three: Make individuals feel like you are talking to them personally

The more that people think that your message relates to them personally, the more they will take notice. Towards the end of the speech, Martin Luther King referenced a number of American states by name, from New York to California. The people living in these states experienced an additional sense of pride and connection to the cause because they could identify with those places when he singled them out. Similarly, JFK talked directly to his audience at Rice University twice during his speech, mentioning how they stood to gain from what he planned to achieve.

Tip four: Speak s-l-o-w-l-y

It should be noted how much a quick pace of speech can *distract* from the message at hand. It becomes harder to concentrate on what the person is saying, as it takes time to digest their message.

Listen to the pace that Martin Luther King used when he delivered a speech. His background as a Baptist minister had given him training in delivering impactful messages. As he spoke, you could almost imagine that King was delivering a sermon in church and could feel the gravitas of his authority.

Tip five: Tell stories

The human brain is wired up to remember stories. Fascinatingly, it's much easier to remember stories than a list of facts. Just reflect back on some of the stories that you have read in this book so far and you will probably find them relatively easy to remember.

People also find stories interesting and if you can weave in a sense of emotion too, they become even more powerful. In addition to our brains being wired up to remember stories, they are also primed to remember emotional events (it makes evolutionary sense to be able to remember both really good things and really bad things), so the more emotion you can weave in, the more memorable your speech will become.

Tip six: Less is more

In the words of Dorothy Sarnoff, 'Make sure you have finished speaking before your audience has finished listening.' Perhaps this is the right place to end this chapter!

 Speaking in public is one of the most powerful things you can do as a leader. Use the right recipe and technique and your speeches will forge motivated followers.

D: Decide Your Strategy

*The leader is the organization's top strategist,
systematically envisioning the future and specifically
mapping out how to get there.*
– Bill Hybells

Deciding your strategy requires you to answer some fundamental questions:

1. Where do you want to be in the future? (i.e. your vision)

2. What do you need to survive in the short term? (e.g. during your start-up phase)

3. What barriers exist that could hinder you from achieving your vision?

4. What strengths do you have which can help you to achieve your vision?

5. What strategies should you adopt to overcome barriers, play to your strengths and move towards the achievement of your vision?

We'll explore these questions through a case study of one of the most outstanding business turnarounds in history – Apple computers.

CASE STUDY

When Steve Jobs retook the reins of Apple in 1997 the company was virtually bankrupt. By the time Jobs died of pancreatic cancer fourteen years later, Apple had become the second most valuable corporation in the world behind Exxon Mobil. So let's unpick the strategy that kicked off this amazing business success and how Jobs' contributed personally to its success.

1. Where do you want to be in the future?

As we said in Chapter A: 'Aspiration', leaders need to have a clear vision of where they want to be in the future. At the Macworld Expo in 1997, an annual trade show dedicated to Apple products, Jobs clearly articulated what he was there to do – 'To make Apple healthy again.'

At first glance, a vision to avoid bankruptcy and improve profits and market share might not seem that inspiring. However, Jobs provided a beacon of hope for the employees who feared for their jobs and for fans who passionately loved the brand. His words were received with rapturous applause from the audience.

In the previous chapter we talked about the importance of compelling communication – part of the reason why Jobs was such an amazing leader was because of his outstanding skills as an orator. You just have to watch a few minutes of Jobs delivering keynote speeches and you feel inspired by what Apple can achieve. Remember when you announce your strategy, it isn't just *what* you say, but *how* you say it, that can make a big difference in terms of securing buy-in.

2. What do you need to survive in the short term?

Having worked out the vision, you then need to plan the first steps towards achieving it. However, as we said in Chapter B: 'Backing', a brilliant idea is worthless if you can't afford to bring it to fruition. Since it takes time to achieve results and Apple was close to bankruptcy, time was running out for Jobs.

At the Macworld Expo in 1998, Jobs explained how he had taken inspiration from Maslow's 'hierarchy of needs'. Maslow's theory states that before a person can achieve anything, they need to ensure that their basic needs are met – water, oxygen, food, shelter, etc. In other words, you need to focus on basic survival. Jobs explained that his first priority had been to ensure the *basic survival* of Apple, which came in the form of a $150 million investment from Microsoft. This had given the lifeline that Apple needed to continue operations – it had pumped fresh blood into its veins. With the backing achieved, Jobs could now focus on the strategy to turn Apple around.

The announcement of the partnership with Microsoft at the Macworld Expo was greeted with the sound of boos from the audience, who were not impressed by Apple's partnership with their greatest rival. Jobs was a strong enough leader to look beyond the initial resistance and do what was required for the greater good of the company. Sometimes your decisions may not be popular, but if you know your decision is right, you need to stand firm.

3. What barriers exist that could hinder you from achieving your vision?

It is important for leaders to be realistic about factors that are holding themselves, their organizations and their people back, so it is critical to identify what is currently not working. Jobs identified three key barriers that were choking Apple.

Firstly, Jobs understood that it is crucial that the right people are in place to lead an organization, particularly through tough times. It was therefore agreed that, due to the financial state Apple was in, it was time for a change of leadership. So the existing board of directors resigned, retaining just two former members and appointing four new ones, including Steve Jobs.

The second key problem was a lack of clear direction, which was leading to employees creating a plethora of products, often badly. It says it all that in an article we read entitled 'Top Ten Apple Products That Flopped', seven out of the top ten items identified were launched between 1993 and 1997. For example, one of the products listed was the Macintosh TV (a computer combined with a television). Although this sounds like a good idea in principle, the machine took forever to boot up, especially compared to switching on a television, and the picture quality was poor. Are you reading this thinking, 'I would have really wanted one of them?' No? We didn't think so.

Thirdly, Apple's diverse product offerings reduced their focus on their core customers. This meant that the company was losing market share in the areas it was *still* doing well in.

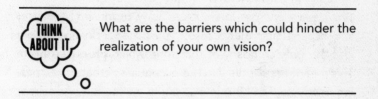

What are the barriers which could hinder the realization of your own vision?

4. What strengths are there which could help to achieve your vision?

In Chapter B: 'Backing', we also stressed the benefits of playing to your strengths and Jobs was focused on understanding what assets Apple had and how to capitalize upon them. Although Apple was failing, Jobs identified that it had three major strengths to play to.

Firstly, Apple computers were clear favourites for creative professionals (i.e. people working in advertising, publishing and design). In 1997, a whopping 80 per cent of creative professionals worked on an Apple Macintosh computer and 64 per cent of all websites were created on a Mac.

Apple's second major strength lay in education. In 1997, Apple was the single largest supplier to education in the world, providing 60 per cent of all computers in schools and 64 per cent of all teachers worked on a Mac.

Jobs also believed that Apple had a great asset to sell – the Mac OS – the operating system of the Macintosh computer. In 1997, there were over 20 million active users of the Mac OS, with a software industry built around it worth half a billion US dollars.

Finally, Apple had a unique competitive advantage. While some competitors, such as Sony, produced hardware, and others, such as Microsoft, produced software, Apple was the only company at that time which produced both. This meant that Apple had the potential to create outstanding products that no one else could make. Plus, if desired, Apple could produce software products that were *only* compatible with their own products. As Jobs described it, this created a 'walled garden' for Apple.

What strengths do you or your organization have which can support the achievement of your vision?

5. What strategies should you adopt to overcome barriers, play to the strengths available and move towards the achievement of the vision?

Having analysed Apple's strengths and weaknesses, Jobs announced the strategy which would be followed to make Apple healthy again:

- New leadership – there were new appointments made to the board of directors.

- Focus on relevance – don't try to produce everything for everyone, instead focus on their core markets. They dramatically reduced their product range to just four products: a laptop computer and a desktop computer, one each for the professional market (e.g. for creative professionals) and one each for the consumer market (e.g. education).

- Invest in core assets – make their greatest asset, the Mac OS, even better. Focus on doing the few things you do to an outstanding quality.

- Meaningful partnerships – referring to the partnership with Microsoft in 1997.

- New product paradigms – taking advantage of their unique competitive advantage to make combined software and hardware products.

This strategy was summarized in a mission statement: 'to provide relevant, compelling, solutions that customers can only get from Apple.'

The strategy quickly had an impact. Between 1997 and 1998, the market value of Apple had more than doubled and profits began to increase each quarter.

Over time, as Apple got healthier and healthier according to Jobs' vision, its strategy evolved and their product range diversified. You can see how powerful some of these strategic principles that Jobs applied to Apple continue to be to this day. New product paradigms continue to lie at the heart of Apple's phenomenal success as demonstrated by the iMac, iPod, iPhone and iPad. The popularity and range of these innovative products mean that Apple is growing their market share in a way that would have seemed impossible before Jobs' 1997 return.

A final tip – keep it simple!

Prior to co-founding Apple in 1976, Steve Jobs spent seven months travelling around India. During this time, he became deeply inspired by Buddhism and felt particularly enlightened by the Buddhist philosophy of simplicity, learning to believe that it was the ultimate sophistication.

You can see how core the principle of simplicity was to Apple's 1997 strategy, when he vastly reduced Apple's product range. It was also a philosophy that infected Apple's product design. Steve Jobs was often heard asking questions such as 'Do we really need that button?', 'Can't you get rid of that step in the interface?' and 'How can we make it more intuitive?'

Simplicity was a key part of Steve Jobs' mantra: 'Simple can be harder than complex: You have to work hard to get your thinking clean to make it simple. But it's worth it in the end because once you get there, you can move mountains.'

When developing your strategy, remember Steve Jobs' philosophy and the principle that less is more. When a vision is clear and the strategy to achieve it is obvious and direct, you stand a far greater chance of success.

 Using your analysis of strengths and weaknesses, and the principle of 'keep it simple', reflect on the strategy you can use to move towards the achievement of your own goal.

 In order to achieve your vision and survive in the short term you will need to decide your strategy; focusing on your core strengths and using them to overcome the barriers that will hold you back.

E: Execute

Doing is a quantum leap from imagining.
– Barbara Sher

You've crystallized your vision, secured the backing needed to launch it and have communicated your intention. You've got a strategy and are confident about the output that you have to deliver. It's now time to make it happen!

In order to execute initiatives in a sound and structured way, leaders need to:

- Appoint key personnel to lead the delivery

- Confirm that your early planning assumptions are correct

- Break the overall output down into key deliverables

- Sequence activities and confirm timelines

- Manage your resources

- Set the minimum acceptable standards and monitor them.

We will look at each of these aspects using an impressive case study – the creation of a stunning artificial island, named Palm Jumeirah, off the coast of Dubai. The island is shaped like a palm tree, is one of the largest artificial islands in the world and is made entirely of reclaimed sand with a rock breakwater.

Type 'Palm Jumeirah' into a search engine and take a look at a picture of the island. You'll see why it has been nicknamed 'The eighth wonder of the world.'

The Palm Jumeirah was the idea of the then Crown Prince, Sheikh Mohammed, in 2000, who had a vision to make Dubai the number one luxury tourist destination in the world and triple the number of visitors from 5 to 15 million per year. However, there was a key problem – the Dubai coastline was only 37 miles long and therefore was not large enough to absorb the increased population. Dubai needed to find a way to increase its coastline, and creating an artificial island was deemed to be the solution.

So how do you create something so impressive out of absolutely nothing?

1. Appoint key personnel to lead the delivery
We recently worked with a group of senior leaders who were working towards delivering a major project. During

a review exercise, the leaders were asked to identify which factors had underpinned the success of their work to date. A theme that came up time and time again was 'recruitment of good people'. If you devote time and energy to hiring the best, the work is more likely to take care of itself.

Strong leaders are not afraid to hire people with more capability than them. They realize that hiring the best will increase their own personal reputation through optimal output.

During the construction of Palm Jumeirah, sponsors were keen to find the very best engineers on the planet to lead the project. Having scoured the world, they appointed Dutch experts who could apply their wealth of expertise in land reclamation from the Netherlands to the Dubai project.

 Make a list of the key roles needed to carry out your initiative. For each role, list the essential qualities and experience needed by the role holder required for them to be highly successful in your project.

---

2. Confirm that your early planning assumptions are correct

Before embarking, it is wise to check your initial assumptions are correct, particularly if they were made prior to the full expert team coming on board.

For example, the Dubai project initiators had made the assumption that it was possible to protect the sand island by a rock breakwater; however, prior to actually building it, much more detailed research was needed to firm up the details of how exactly this would work. What were the worst possible weather conditions the area could be subjected to? How far away from the island did the break-water need to be, and what height of barrier was required to offer enough protection from that worst-case weather scenario? Failure to address these concerns adequately at the design stage could lead to catastrophic consequences later on.

Although there is often a sense of urgency around new initiatives and a hunger to make progress, time is initially best invested in up-front planning. Plans can be easily changed, however, work that has already been started will be harder and more costly to modify. While being mindful of the overall deadline, leaders should not mistake plan-ning for inactivity – take heed from the words of Benjamin Franklin: 'By failing to prepare, you are preparing to fail.'

3. Break the overall output down into key deliverables

It is helpful to break the overall goal into a series of project deliverables in order to more easily manage and control their delivery.

For example, the construction of Palm Jumeirah was split into three key phases:

(i) The creation of a breakwater island, to enclose the palm-shaped island and provide protection from severe storm waves and tidal surges.

(ii) Construction of the palm-shaped island itself. This land mass was to be made entirely from sand and needed to be solid enough to support a city infrastructure, remain stable over time (e.g. surviving earthquakes) and required an accurate shaping.

(iii) Building of the city and its infrastructure and utilities, to supply housing, hotels and commercial outlets.

Once you have identified the high-level deliverables, you can then subdivide each one further to detail the specific activities that must be completed. For example:

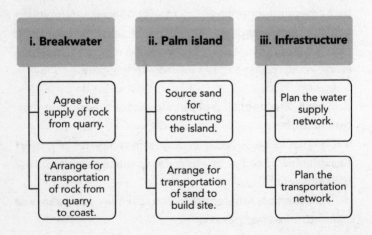

You should be able to summarize all key deliverables and sub-activities onto an A4 sheet of paper.

- Identify the key deliverables required to achieve a major goal.

- Brainstorm sub-activities for each key deliverable onto sticky notes (one activity per sticky note).

- Aim to summarize the output onto a single sheet of A4 paper.

---

4. Sequence activities and confirm timelines

Once you have a clear idea of the required deliverables, the next step is to identify the sequence in which activities will take place, based on their interdependences.

For example, before the palm-shaped island could be built above sea level, 600ft of the breakwater wall had to be completed or the sand would wash away. Prior to any infrastructure being laid, it was essential that the sand had been thoroughly compacted by machinery. Since the first units were due to be handed over to their owners in 2006, and builders required two years to lay the infrastructure, the island had to be ready for construction by the end of 2004.

In order to create a proposed sequence of activities you need to:

- Estimate how long each key activity will take

- Identify which steps must be completed prior to commencing an activity

- Identify any critical activities that must be started/completed by a certain date (or the project will fail/overrun)

- Agree which activities can be moved or extended without causing an issue

- Plan in contingency time, to compensate for inevitable unforeseen delays.

 Take one deliverable line of notes from the previous activity and put them into a sequence for completion. Write deadline dates on the sticky notes for completing each activity. Repeat this with the other key deliverables and create an overall plan.

---

5. Manage your resources

Projects require resources – money, human effort, tools, materials, etc. Once you know what activities need to be completed, you can identify what resources are needed to achieve them. Costly delays can occur when resources aren't well managed.

The Dubai team managed to create an exceptionally slick operation. They hired thousands of construction workers. They gathered the tools needed to build the sea wall – barges, tugboats, dredgers, floating cranes and land-based machines. And they sourced 7.2 million cubic yards of rock from sixteen quarries across the UAE – enough to build two Egyptian pyramids. Quarry workers blasted rock night and day, loaded it onto trucks, drove it to the coast, placed it on ships and onto the breakwater – all within 24 hours of the initial rock blast. Similar efficiency was achieved during the construction of the sand island, dredging sand from the sea and spraying it in place night and day.

The proactive attitude to managing resources was critical. One employee commented on the philosophy in the team. If something was coming from overseas, they didn't just wait for it to arrive if it was late, they got on the plane and proactively chased it.

Note that, when managing an intensive operation, it is absolutely critical that you treat your people well and make sure their welfare needs are met. For more information on this, please see our sister book in this series: *Introducing Management – A Practical Guide.*

 Make a list of the major resources that you will need to complete your project. Are there any key deadlines by which resources need to be in place in order to meet your key delivery dates?

---

6. Set the minimum acceptable standards and monitor them

Defining what *standards* the work should meet is an important aspect of leading people to deliver, enabling them to work efficiently and ultimately creating output that is both good enough and on time.

For some tasks the 80:20 rule may apply, in other words that 80 per cent of the benefit is achieved through the first 20 per cent of effort. After that, the law of diminishing returns kicks in, therefore leaders should help people to understand *when good is good enough*, enabling people to maximize their productivity.

There will also be times when nothing less than 100 per cent perfect will do, so, leaders need to clearly define when time *is* going to be well spent going that extra mile and aiming for perfection. During the construction of the rock breakwater, it was absolutely essential that the breakwater blocks were free from cracks, otherwise the whole structure could become vulnerable. Diving teams painstakingly checked every block – quality sampling would not be enough when nothing less than 100 per cent perfection would do.

With regard to your project or work:

- What tasks must be completed to an exceptionally high standard?

- Where can you best apply the 80:20 rule?

The culmination of massive effort

You can imagine the mass of activity required to heave the breakwater rocks from the quarry to the sea and dredge 60 million cubic metres of sand from the sea bed, transport it to the construction site and spray it into place in the perfect shape of a palm tree. Once the sand island had been completed, 20,000 labourers then moved in to install the infrastructure of the island – gas, electricity, water supply, sewerage systems and buildings. Their task was to build an entire city at sea in just two years. After a monumental effort, as promised, the developers announced the first units were ready for completion in 2006.

 In order to execute your strategy you need the right people in place, undertaking the right deliverables efficiently at the right time, while ensuring the assumptions in your plan are correct and that work is being carried out to the required standard.

F: Forming the Team

Coming together is a beginning. Keeping together is progress. Working together is success.
– Henry Ford

Henry Ford, founder of the Ford Motor Company and inventor of the manufacturing assembly line, was a great advocate of teamwork.

Prior to the use of the assembly line, highly skilled craftsmen would build products in isolation from start to finish and their output was very slow. However, Ford realized that the process could be dramatically sped up by individuals working on an individual task, then passing their output to a colleague to build upon. This process was repeated in an efficient order, over and over again, until the whole product had been completed. Through working as a team, Ford was able to reduce the time taken to build a car from weeks to just six hours.

Ford had demonstrated the principle **T**ogether **E**veryone **A**chieves **M**ore.

When you consider the fast pace that the modern-day world works at, you can understand why it is so important for teams to work slickly together. Just reflect back upon the construction of Palm Jumeirah and consider how important it was for the team to operate like a well-oiled machine, with individual cogs interacting seamlessly with each other.

Add to that the fact that it would actually be impossible to achieve many visions in isolation anyway – for example, Walt Disney could not have built Disneyland on his own and Gandhi and Martin Luther King needed an army of motivated followers behind them to make governments sit up and take notice.

So teamwork is critical if you want to efficiently achieve a vision. This chapter therefore looks at how leaders can bring their teams together and inspire them to work together in harmony.

Coming together is a beginning ...

When a new team forms, one of the key foundations of success is for team members to get to know each other, personally and professionally.

Personal introductions

You will know from your own experience that even if you've just had a short conversation with a new colleague, the next time you see them or when you need to work with them, the ice has already been broken. So it can be helpful for leaders to engineer situations where team members greet each other on a one-to-one basis.

While there are many different exercises to facilitate personal introductions, one of the most effective that we've used has been 'speed meeting'. Set people up in pairs and give them one minute to chat about anything they like. At the end of the minute, blow a whistle and get team members to find a new partner. Repeat as many times as you like. We've found that teams typically really enjoy this activity and it is quick and easy to do.

Professional introductions

This often involves gaining a high-level understanding of what other people's job roles are and how they connect to the bigger picture of the team. To make this type of exercise fun, leaders can give their team members coloured pens and paper and ask them (either individually or by subteams) to draw a picture to represent what success looks like for their individual contribution. Team members should then talk each other through the pictures. This enables the team to succinctly share knowledge about each other's job roles, their skills and how they fit into the overall operation.

Keeping together is progress ...

Combatting silo mentality

Leaders can often suffer from the problem of silo mentality – in other words people refusing to help each other across jobs, teams or departments because 'That's not my job.' You could face a situation where some people are struggling to deliver, while others watch smugly from the sidelines thinking how much better they are at their jobs. Worse still, conflict can arise between individuals and groups battling over resources, arguing about who needs or deserves them more.

What people fail to realize is that this type of behaviour is simply like shooting yourself in the foot. When team members are ultimately supposed to be working to achieve a common goal, if one part fails to contribute, the whole team is being let down. And in some cases, the result of this is that the whole team fails.

Take a moment to consider Henry Ford's assembly line. It didn't matter how well an individual worker completed his own component, if he wasn't on time or others failed to complete their job, the complete car could not be produced. It took the whole team to work together cohesively to create a shared success.

A great way to break down silo mentality is to highlight the web of interdependency that exists within in the team. To do this:

- Give each team member three sticky notes and ask them to 'Look around the room and choose three people within this wider team who can support you to do your job better.'

- Write the names of those three people on the three sticky notes (one name per sticky note) and then, underneath each name, write down what that person can do to support you.

- Then ask the team members to mingle around the room and stick the note to the people who they wrote about, at the same time verbally telling them what they can do to help.

This exercise reinforces the message that success is

dependent upon each other as well as demonstrating how people can support one another and build connections. Some people will also end up covered in sticky notes, which is a very visual way of showing key dependencies within the team.

Agreeing the rules of play

Where leaders are faced with undesired behaviour within the team, it can reflect badly on everyone and can detract from the good work that is happening. To avoid this, it can be powerful to get the team to draw up the 'rules of play'. This was a strategy adopted by Sir Clive Woodward as he led the England team to compete in the 2003 Rugby World Cup.

When new members joined the team, a notebook of rules was issued as part of the uniform, such was the importance of this item to the team's success. Being part of the team and wearing the uniform entailed also signing up to the team's self-generated rules.

To create a rule, Clive would suggest a topic of interest to his players, such as their conduct when eating together in public, and would then leave the room. The players would then be free to discuss their own opinions on what would be acceptable and unacceptable. Their task was to define their own rules (essentially their united behavioural standards), for example, always wearing a tie when dining as a team in public. Once the team were happy with their rules, they would present them to Clive.

On the face of it, this may not seem that different to other team rules for exercises that you may have heard of or participated in in the past, however, there were two subtle but extremely powerful differences in the way that Clive executed this activity.

Firstly, 100 per cent of the team had to commit to the rule. Ninety per cent wasn't good enough. Why? Because once *one* person's standards start slipping, it is easy for the whole team to also slide into bad ways. So having *everyone* signed up to behaving in a certain way was key. Also, since every member of the team had personally agreed to the behavioural standard, it would make it more difficult for them to opt out in future.

A second key difference was that, as the leader, Clive gave himself the right to veto the newly generated team rules. If he didn't agree with the proposed rule, then he would request the team to discuss it further until it had his buy-in. This was helpful since, although the team themselves were being empowered, the leader did not abdicate his responsibility.

Once 100 per cent of the team (including the leader) were signed up to the rule it would be written in the book and would become a behaviour expected of all members of the team. Over time, more and more rules were added and, occasionally, rules were reviewed to check that they were still relevant and that new members of the team were on board too.

THINK ABOUT IT How much more likely are team members to commit to a rule that they have developed themselves versus a rule that they are being required to comply with?

 In psychological terms, there is a significant difference between compliance and commitment. If you simply tell someone to do something, they may comply because they have to, however, if they aren't naturally rule-abiding or they don't agree with the edict, you risk non-compliance. Therefore, where possible, leaders should aim to achieve commitment – in other words make people act in a desirable way because they *want* to. Consultation is an effective way to achieve commitment to decisions, since people who shape solutions are likely to accept them, as long as the final outcome genuinely takes on board their input.

Working together is success

The whole team has to put effort in to achieve a vision

Team members will often know what success looks like, however, actually achieving it is another matter and often requires everyone to actively play their part to realize success.

You can illustrate this point in a powerful way using a long (approximately 10ft) bamboo cane (aka the helium stick!) and approximately ten people.

- Place the bamboo cane on the floor and ask the group to gather either side of the stick, with half the participants on one side and half on the other.

- Ask participants to make a gun shape with both of their hands apart (i.e. extend their first and middle fingers), then turn their hands up, so the palms are facing the ceiling.

- Explain that you will shortly rest the stick on people's fingers and that the object of the exercise will be to lower the stick to the floor from a standing position. The only rule is that all participants' fingers must remain in contact with the stick at all times.

- Pick up the helium stick and place it on the upturned fingers.

- The stick will mysteriously rise and the group will be baffled. It can often take about twenty minutes to complete this simple task – some teams never manage to lower the stick to the ground!

People will ask you whether the stick is magic! If you want to explain the truth, this simple but somewhat mind-blowing exercise works because the upwards pressure exerted on the stick by people's fingers is greater than the downward pressure caused by the weight of the stick, therefore gravity is defied (as if by magic!).

After the exercise, you can ask your team what they learnt from doing the exercise. A great point to draw out during team building is the fact that sometimes everyone *knows* what the team needs to achieve, however, it takes everyone to work together and to put in *effort* to actually realize that vision. Knowing what you need to do is not the same as actually doing it. Once everybody is pulling in exactly the same direction, the team can achieve success.

Give some of these exercises a go with your team, during a team meeting or training day. People will enjoy the activities and you can use them to highlight key behaviours to the team.

In the words of Helen Keller (author, political activist and the first deaf-blind person to earn a Bachelor of Arts degree), 'Alone we can do so little, together we can do so much.' Between 1908 and October 1927, the Ford Motor Company produced over 15 million Model T cars and transformed the car industry for ever. In 2003, Clive Woodward's team made their nation cheer as they won the final of the Rugby World Cup. When teams gel cohesively, great things can happen.

The success of a team is dependent upon every person within that team achieving what's required of them. To do that the leader needs to ensure that they come together, keep together and work together.

G: Guiding Values

*It's not hard to make decisions when you know
what your values are.*
– Roy Disney

Values guide behaviour

Think about your own personal values – the things that are important to you. If you're someone who values status, you are more likely to want to drive a flashy car than someone who has no desire for visible signs of wealth. If you value learning, you will be more likely to jump at the chance to undertake a new qualification than someone who hates studying and thinks that it is pointless.

Values are significant because they subconsciously shape our behaviour on a day-to-day basis. People find it hard to go against their values – for example, if you believe in the importance of rules and regulations, you will be much more likely to stick to the speed limit when you drive.

The word *subconscious* is important, because people don't typically think, 'Hey, I don't value rules, I'm going to jump a red light today!' – they simply do it. Yet the underlying value is constantly present, guiding their behaviour as much when driving a car as it is when the alarm clock goes off and you press the snooze button ('I can be late today, it doesn't matter!').

Values are interesting because everyone has their own unique combination. So when it comes to working together, a team of people are very *unlikely* to be singing from the same hymn sheet. This can prove a problem for leaders since it leads to inconsistent behaviour – for example, some people may naturally follow the rules and adhere to an organizational dress code, whereas others will tend to be more lax. When people are driven by different values, and therefore demonstrate different behaviour, it can become a source of friction within teams.

Organizational values

To harmonize the myriad of personal values, astute organizations live and promote *organizational values* to guide behaviour across the whole entity. Used well, values infect the culture of an organization, positively impacting everyday decisions and actions.

Since values aim to channel behaviour in the *same* direction, leaders need to ensure that behaviour is channelled in the *right* direction. Therefore values should be aligned with the organization's vision and mission.

In Chapter A: 'Aspiration', we explained that your vision is *where you aspire to be in future*, and your mission is *what you aspire to do, at your best, every day*. Values add meat onto the bones of how the mission and vision will be achieved.

REMEMBER THIS!!! The vision harmonizes the organization in terms of *where* it is headed; the mission harmonizes *what* people are striving to achieve; and values harmonize *how* people should act.

CASE STUDY Organizational values are extremely important to the smoothie company we mentioned in Chapter B: 'Backing'. Innocent Drinks (now known as 'Innocent') grew from a start-up operation in 1999 to making a profit of over £3.5 million within just a few years.

Innocent's purpose (mission) is 'To make natural, delicious food and drink that helps people to live well and die old'. In 2007, Innocent stated its vision: 'To be the Earth's favourite little food company', a goal which is heavily underpinned by the organization's desire to be a world leader in terms of sustainability. The mission and vision are underpinned by five key values:

- Be natural – aim to produce 100 per cent natural products and to 'be yourself' at work.

- Be entrepreneurial – chase every opportunity and be as responsive as possible.

- Be responsible – think about the consequences of actions in both the short and long term.

- Be commercial – aim for growth and profit, being tough but fair.

- Be generous – with feedback, time, rewards and charitable support.

Like many organizations, the company's values stemmed from the beliefs of its founders – Richard Reed, Adam Balon and Jon Wright. Values can then be sustained through recruiting people whose own personal values naturally align to those of the organization.

The stronger and more visible the values, the more they shape behaviour. The values are very strong at Innocent – you can see its values and aligned vision and mission being woven into the fabric of everyday culture at company headquarters, Fruit Towers, in London:

- To encourage people to be themselves (i.e. 'be natural'), employees are free to work communally or in a more private space, and can walk around barefoot if they please!

- The office carpet is made of fake grass, to remind employees of the importance of nature and because it was good value for money, i.e. made good commercial sense.

- Fruit Towers is run using green energy, tapping into the value 'be responsible'.

- Innocent generously donates 10 per cent of all its profits each year to the Innocent Foundation, which funds community-based projects in the countries from which it sources its fruit.

 You are an employee at Innocent and you have come up with a suggestion related to the organization's forthcoming office move to larger premises. Your idea is to recycle as much of the old office's furniture as possible for re-use in the new building, thereby avoiding using new materials and having more costs. Based on the organization's vision, mission and values, do you think that your proactive suggestion will be welcomed?

Innocent *did* indeed recycle as much as it possibly could during its office relocation. Hopefully from this example you can see how everyday decisions and behaviour can be guided by values and their overarching mission and vision.

Making values live

Leaders need to ensure that the desired behaviours that are linked to values are actually practised on a day-to-day basis. For example, it's no good having 'sustainability' as a core way of working if everyone constantly prints out page after page of a document and jokes that they need to hide the evidence from the 'sustainability police'. So how can leaders make their precious values 'live'? Here are some ideas:

- Cover values in your induction – from day one (if not before!) let employees know what your values are and why they are important to the overall mission and vision of the organization.

- Sign up to values – provide a values board for all new employees to sign when they join the organization, signalling that they commit to living the values. It's very powerful and motivating to find your name on a values board among your fellow employees.

- Reward people who role-model living the values – remember, what gets recognized gets done. Some companies assess values as part of a formal appraisal process and bonus payments are given to people who have demonstrated the values. Other companies give on-the-spot bonus prizes for people who have done something outstanding to make a value live.

- Plaster your values everywhere – and that means doing far more than putting a shiny plaque in reception!

- Finally, visibly weave the practice of values into everyday working – as we'll see in Chapter S: 'Set an example', if leaders 'walk the talk', their people will soon follow.

A test to determine whether or not your values are prominent enough is to ask people to name them on demand. If they can't, you need to work harder to bring them to life.

 Name all of your organization's values!

What other ways can leaders bring values to life?

 Values help to guide decisions. The stronger your values, and the more aligned they are to your vision, the greater the focus of energy towards a common goal.

H: Help Underperformers

A leader's role is to raise people's aspirations for what they can become and to release their energies so that they will try to get there.
– David Gergen

The next few chapters look at how leaders' actions can bring out the best (and the worst!) in their people's performance, starting first with the impact leaders can have when individuals are struggling to succeed.

We used to be of the opinion that if a business leader wanted to reap good performance from their people, the two key things that they needed to focus on were:

- Hiring strong people
- Keeping these people motivated.

We have now modified this viewpoint, since previously we failed to take into account the potential of a person to develop from a weak performer to an exceptional one, given the right support and conditions.

This shift in point of view occurred when we attended a leadership conference and realized that leaders are like watering cans. It doesn't matter if a seedling is strong or weak, given the right conditions and attention they can enable growth against all odds.

We later read a tear-jerking story called 'Three letters from Teddy' which further cemented this view.

Type 'Teddy Stallard and Mrs Thompson' into an internet search engine and read this inspiring tale.

In a nutshell, the story centres upon a schoolboy named Teddy Stallard, who had become an outcast of his class. He was failing in school, he was mocked by others for being dirty and smelly. As the story unfolded, his teacher, Miss Thompson, discovered that the deterioration in Teddy's well-being and academic performance was linked to the death of his mother. It was inspiring to read how a leader (in this case the teacher) was able to transform the performance of an individual, simply by changing her own attitude and behaviour. Teddy was able to go on and become a doctor.

When someone is struggling, time, attention and a helping hand can provide a crucial turning point, allowing a person's confidence and ability to improve to a point where they can begin to shine.

This inspirational story about Teddy Stallard is actually fictional – written by a lady called Elizabeth Silance Ballard in the 1970s for a magazine called *Home Life*. However, it is interesting to compare this magical piece of writing to a real-life fairy tale, now immortalized by the film *The Blind Side* which followed the life of an American teenager called Michael Oher.

The life of Michael Oher

Michael Oher had come from a very troubled background – his father was murdered and his mother was a drug addict. Sadly, much of his childhood was spent fending for himself and running away from foster care homes.

However, 2002 was a turning point for Michael when, as a young teenager, he was fortunate to be temporarily taken under the wing of a local community member called Tony Henderson. Tony was trying to get his own son enrolled at the local Christian school and, in a positive twist of fate, he was able to enrol Michael at the same time.

Over the next few years, Michael remained homeless, living between families at the school, continuing to find shelter wherever he could, until eventually a family called the Tuohy family generously opened their door to him. They offered him a more permanent home, which eventually led to them legally adopting him.

Michael's story is a true rags-to-riches tale. He worked his way up from being a homeless teenager with abysmal school grades and a background perilously close to gang culture to become a college graduate and top American football player who signed a multi-million dollar contract with the Baltimore Ravens in 2009.

Listening to interviews with Michael, it's obvious that he deserves much personal credit for the success he has achieved in life. He clearly was determined to make something more of his life than he was born into. However it is also useful to explore how the people around him helped him to flourish.

Rent and watch a copy of *The Blind Side*. Be sure to have a box of tissues to hand!

So how can leaders help struggling individuals to thrive? Let's take a look at some of the things that you could be doing.

Ensure that basic needs are met

As we explained in Chapter D: 'Decide your strategy', according to Maslow's hierarchy of needs (and common sense), in the immediate context, it is impossible to focus on self-improvement activities when you have more pressing basic needs to be met, such as finding food or shelter for the night. You can see in the case of Michael Oher, being homeless detracted from his ability to focus upon his education and get good grades at school. When the Tuohy family took him in, they enabled Michael to have these needs met.

Maslow divides basic needs into two categories – physiological needs (the literal requirements for survival such as water, sleep, breathing and sanitary needs) and safety needs (freedom from physical or mental harm). When a person seems to be distracted, it may be a sign that their basic needs are not being met.

Where these basic needs are not being met, leaders should identify the most appropriate course of action to resolve the deficiency:

- It may be your organization's responsibility to resolve the issue – for example if someone is repeatedly absent and you find out that this is due to bullying, you will need to investigate the issue and take disciplinary action if appropriate.

- In other instances, the deficiency in needs falls outside your boundary of responsibility to solve. In this case you should identify the most suitable person/body who could help and question whether it is appropriate or not for you to highlight it to them, being aware of any duty of care responsibilities that you have. It might be that the person actually experiencing the deficiency is the most appropriate person to resolve the issue – for example, if someone is constantly tired, they may be able to change their sleeping patterns themselves.

Provide additional support
A struggling performer may need additional support to help them to catch up. Michael Oher benefitted from the support of a home tutor who helped him to dramatically increase his

grade point average. In the 'Three letters from Teddy' story, the teacher provided extra instruction to Teddy at the time when he needed academic support the most.

When providing additional support, you are likely to be far more successful if the person you are assisting has bought into the *why* ('Why do I need to do this?') and the *how* ('How can we best achieve our goal?'). Michael Oher was motivated to create a better future for himself, so the additional support was welcomed to help him qualify for the football scholarship and realize his potential.

In contrast, if someone is not even interested in trying, providing additional support might be the same as throwing resources down the drain. In this situation, try to find a motivational hook, which will give them more of an incentive. What is it that they *do* want to achieve? Aim to link their efforts to that goal.

Inspire a person that you believe they can do it

A key reason why people can resist support is because they don't believe that they can improve – they think that there is no point in trying, it just won't make any difference. This is a tricky situation; how do you get someone to believe that they can do something that they don't believe that they can do?

Think of a time when you managed to do something (big or small) that previously you believed was completely and utterly impossible.

This exercise can be very powerful in shifting beliefs about capability. You need to help a person to realize that they *can* do things that they currently believe are impossible, because they've already been able to do this in the past. Shifting to the belief that a future goal is possible is a very important step towards achieving it. After all, if you don't even try, that is a sure way to guarantee you will fail.

A leader's own beliefs can be infectious. Do not underestimate the power of a person in authority believing in you. Sometimes positive encouragement from a leader is all a person needs to take the plunge and go for it. After all, if a leader believes in them, perhaps they can start to believe in themselves.

It can be powerful to get someone to focus on what they *can* do rather than what they can't do. In other words, encourage them to play to their strengths. It is much easier to succeed at things that you are good at than trying to fix weaknesses to begin with, when a person is at their most vulnerable. Playing to a person's strengths builds confidence and self-belief.

Identify someone who is struggling to realize their potential, who you can support to thrive. Commit to take one step, big or small, to make a difference to them.

Refuse to take other people's prejudices on board

Struggling individuals can acquire a negative label which causes others, including leaders, to look upon them with contempt. Worse still, people can develop a siege mentality whereby they collectively mock an 'outcast' and derive a sick sense of satisfaction from seeing them fail. For example, at the beginning of the 'Three letters to Teddy' story the teacher took delight in giving Teddy appalling grades, vindicating her poor opinion of him.

It takes a strong leader to reach out a helping hand to someone rejected by a group or society. Michael Oher was fortunate enough that people in his life could look beyond the negative stereotype of his background and see his potential, and look what he achieved as a result. It only takes one person to start accepting someone and, over time, others will follow.

The next time you hear others mocking someone who is struggling, ask yourself, 'What can I do to help?' and offer a supportive hand. You have the potential to completely transform someone's life.

 Leaders are like watering cans – given the right care and conditions, even the weakest seedlings can thrive. It takes time and energy to support struggling individuals, but persevere, and you'll be amazed at how much they can grow.

I: Inspire Top Performance

*A leader is like a shepherd. He stays behind the flock,
letting the most nimble go out ahead, whereupon the
others follow, not realizing that all along they are being
directed from behind.*
– Nelson Mandela

They say that finding true love can equate to weight gain, and unfortunately for David and I this came true! We both put on around 35lbs during the first three years that we knew each other. D'oh!

Eventually we realized enough was enough, so we changed our eating habits and managed to lose about half of the weight that we had gained. However, we simply couldn't shift the rest, so reluctantly we joined the dreaded gym. Thankfully, attending the gym has been so much better than we had anticipated, largely as a result of attending a wide range of different types of exercise classes, which are infinitely more palatable than just sticking to the treadmill.

We are lucky that the vast majority of staff at our gym lead classes to a very high standard. However, one instructor, Mel, has excelled above everyone else. What's interesting is that Mel executes the class in a pretty standard method to other instructors – so it isn't *what* she is doing that differentiates her. However, the *way* that she leads the class is different, and this helps me to perform at my very best (for which my somewhat flatter stomach is extremely grateful).

So what can we learn from Mel about how leaders can improve their people's performance?

Learn people's names

It might sound like a small thing, but it makes a noticeable difference.

I don't remember meeting the other instructors for the first time, but I do remember meeting Mel. She welcomed me into the class and asked my name, which made a really positive impression. Most other instructors simply ask you to tick your name off on the list and probably don't think to ask what you are actually called.

The next time I came to Mel's class, she welcomed me immediately by name. It really took me by surprise, especially since no other member of staff had previously (or since) referred to me as 'Alison'. Eight months after we first met, Mel still uses my name every time we meet and it makes me feel valued – it's difficult to feel that a leader cares about your performance if they don't even know your name.

In the past, I worked with a training company who prided itself on getting great scores on its post-course evaluation forms. They were focused on understanding the factors that can influence the scores, to the point where they identified that supplying sweets in the classroom was a contributory factor – and then refined it to a particular brand of sweets to raise the bar even higher! Interestingly their research also uncovered that referring to everyone in the course by name was enough to positively influence ratings of the course.

Remembering people's names can be difficult, so you may wish to use this memory technique.

When someone tells you their name, try and associate it with something, either someone you know or something about their appearance. For example, imagine that you meet someone called Elizabeth, you might want to think of her wearing a crown and therefore associating her with HM Queen Elizabeth II. The reason this works is because it creates an 'associative memory' (i.e. linking a new fact to something we already know), which is easier to remember than a 'free recall' memory, where we are just trying to remember something in isolation.

Once you've memorized the name, use it a few times in conversation to reinforce the memory further.

Set the standard to the level of the strongest participant

Mel once told me that she aims to deliver a class that will be challenging enough for the strongest participant. Her philosophy is that this raises the performance of other people in the group. If you set the standard to the level of the average participant, then half of the class will not perform to the best of their ability and may feel bored.

In contrast, I attended a class a couple of times that was taught by an instructor who made the session far too easy, even for someone a bit out of shape like me. Having completed the class, I knew that I didn't get much benefit for my time and I left feeling disappointed. There is something satisfying about trying your best and seeing yourself improve, and it can be motivating when someone is stretching you.

Note the difference between the words 'stretch' and 'strain'. When playing to the level of the strongest, you need to be extra vigilant about the weaker participants. I can see that Mel is constantly scanning the class to see how her attendees are feeling. When she can see that someone is struggling, she suggests a range of options, from easy to hard, so people can work out at their own pace. Another course participant recovering from an injury said how comfortable she feels in Mel's class – she feels that the leader is paying attention to her and allowing her to progress at her own pace. She commented how much she enjoys the session and how much she, and her injury, is improving.

Praise people for their efforts or performance

It can be very motivating when leaders notice individual achievements and efforts and give feedback on this. I have noticed that Mel always gives me some individual feedback at the end of the lesson, for example praising me for how hard I tried during the class. This acts as a form of positive reinforcement. The more the leader compliments you for trying hard, the more it can motivate you to try hard, because your efforts are noticed. In contrast, failing to recognize people can have a very negative effect, for example, when companies do not recognize their top performers these people will often leave or stop trying.

A good technique to simultaneously motivate people while raising their standards is to compliment them on what they are doing well and ask them to self-identify what they can do to improve further. Most of the time people already know how to improve themselves, which saves you the need to deliver criticism, or they can at least guess, which opens the door for you to agree or give your opinion on the correction. It works well and is a very positive way of delivering feedback.

There is a saying, 'What gets rewarded gets done' so if you want people to try hard, notice when people are putting in extra effort and let them know you have seen it. The CEO of one company did exactly that, he sent one of his workers a handwritten thank you note for completing her work on a project. It takes pride of place on her desk and continues to pay motivational dividends every time she sees it. Something as simple as a handwritten note of thanks may have only taken the CEO about 30 seconds to write, but it will have an impact on that employee every day.

Demonstrate that you noticed when people weren't there

A heavy workload prevented me from attending the gym for several weeks and when I next saw Mel, she came up to me and said that she'd noticed I hadn't been around. It was nice to feel missed and since then I've been making an extra special effort to attend, which has improved my results as I'm exercising more often.

If you are working for someone and you feel like they don't acknowledge your presence, it can be very demotivating to the point where you can consider not bothering to attend. Since it's impossible to achieve good results if the right people aren't actually present when they are meant to be, it is important for leaders to actively encourage the attendance of their people.

Show concern when people aren't their normal selves

Something negative had happened one day prior to me attending one of Mel's classes. I must have looked a little distracted because at the end of the session, she came and asked me if I was OK. Just the act of being noticed by the 'leader' made me feel better, as I felt valued.

I remember the same feeling at primary school – I could only have been about seven years old and must have been suffering from a headache, which was quite unusual for me. I have a vivid memory of my head teacher, Miss Ball, an exceptionally kind and gentle lady, taking me to her office and taking my temperature. It wasn't her job to do this, but the attention from the leader made me feel much better.

Perhaps there is still a little bit of child left in us all. There is a magical feeling associated with someone in the position of authority noticing how you feel and showing that they care. I think that many of us would admit to trying harder for someone who cares about us. And research backs this up – a global study by McKinsey in 2009 ('Motivating People: Getting Beyond Money') found that attention from leaders was more effective at motivating than a financial reward like a base pay rise!

Great leaders make *everyone* feel like *they* are the most important person

From the above examples, you'll probably understand why Mel has a knack of making me feel like I'm the most special person in the class.

If I'm honest, now that I look, I also see that the things which make me feel good (i.e. praise as I leave, knowing my name, etc.) are also used with everyone else! This is a truly exceptional talent because *everyone* probably feels like they are the most special person in the class and we are all benefitting from our higher performance due to her fantastic leadership style.

 A leader has the ability to get people to try harder and perform better at their roles simply by being attentive, connecting personally and giving them recognition.

J: Joyful Working

If you have fun at what you do, you'll never work a day in your life. Make work like play and play like hell.
– Norman Brinker

- Write down a list of words that you naturally associate with the concept of work.
- Write down a list of words that you naturally associate with the concept of play.

You are likely to have two fairly polarized lists, for example, work might be viewed as *hard, boring* or *tiring*, while the concept of play might conjure up thoughts of *enjoyment, relaxation* and *play*. But does work really have to be limited to a place of hard labour and serious business?

The link between mood and performance

Integrating fun with work is not a revolutionary idea. For example, during the agricultural age, work songs were used to increase productivity while relieving feelings of boredom. The same principle was applied at sea with the concept of the sea shanty – you may have heard of the song 'What Shall We Do With the Drunken Sailor?' which was used to accompany work tasks on ships, particularly those that needed to be carried out at a steady pace. Yet in today's workplace we have spoken to leaders who frown upon the practice of listening to music through headphones while sitting at an office desk, viewing it as unprofessional and distracting.

However, modern-day research reveals that our elders may in fact have been wiser! There is now an increasing body of evidence that proves a link between mood, creativity and productivity.

For example, in 1991, researcher Alice Isen asked doctors to make a series of medical diagnoses based on a set of symptoms. The experiment divided the doctors into three groups:

- One group was simply asked to make a diagnosis.

- The second group made their diagnosis after reading a medical journal to help them to 'warm up'.

- The third group was asked to make their diagnosis after being primed to feel happy (by giving them sweets, which they were not allowed to eat as it would have influenced their blood sugar levels!).

The results of this fascinating study showed that the doctors who were primed to feel happy were able to make a correct medical diagnosis up to 50 per cent more quickly than both of the other groups. They were also able to reach the correct diagnosis in half as many steps!

Similar conclusions have been drawn from studies of four-year-old children completing shapes puzzles. John Masters, Chris Barden and Martin Ford primed half of the kids in the study to feel happy by thinking about their best ever memory and these children completed the puzzle up to 50 per cent more quickly than those who had not been primed. It would appear that the link between mood and productivity is present from at least the age of four, if not from birth.

And linking back to the impact of music on performance, a study from the University of Windsor in Canada found that software developers working without music produced a lower quality and volume of work. In contrast, those who listened to background music reported positive mood changes and enhanced perception while working. Plus, this positive change in mood correlated with increased curiosity, a useful factor when undertaking creative work.

Psychologists have concluded that the link between a positive mood and productivity can be explained by two key factors. Firstly, being in a good mood makes people more resilient to failure – they are more motivated to keep trying when they don't succeed first time. Secondly, as with the study above on music, a positive mood correlated with both the doctors and children adopting more creative strategies to help them to succeed in their tasks. So a positive mood is linked not only to increased productivity, but increased creativity.

Happiness has tangible business benefits

Psychologists are increasingly turning attention to researching the business benefits of having happy employees. The results should be thought-provoking for those who question whether there is a place for fun at work. For example, the Professor of Psychology at the University of California Riverside, Sonja Lyubomirsky, has found that happy employees:

- Are more productive

- Are less likely to experience job burnout

- Have less time off sick

- Have higher levels of creativity

- Have higher levels of resilience

- Generate more sales.

If you'd like to reap some of these rewards, it's worth thinking about ways to make your employees feel happier, one of which is through encouraging people to have more fun at work.

How to create a more playful working environment

Google has thrown the traditional concept of the workplace environment out of the window and has created a very different workplace. Here's just a flavour of the perks that 'Googlers' can enjoy at their head office in California:

- A video games room

- Relaxation areas with napping pods

- Tiki bars where you can grab a drink with friends

- Four on-site gyms that can be accessed any time of day

- Fifteen restaurants providing free food throughout the day, cooked by world-class chefs

- Massage facilities, with a free treatment on your birthday

- The opportunity to bring your dog to the office

- An on-site laundry, enabling you to bring your dirty laundry to work and pick it up clean.

All of this is provided in an environment where the dress code dictates that anything goes, from pyjamas to roller blades! The showers, laundry facilities, food and sleeping areas mean that it is possible to exist at the Google's HQ for a number of days, with all basic needs being met. If we offered you the opportunity to stay at your place of work for days on end, would you feel so keen?

Given the perks listed above, plus the additional working practices you'll read about later in Chapter M:

'Motivate', it's obvious why *Fortune* magazine has named Google among the top five companies to work for every year it has published its list – since 2007, including naming them as winners in 2007, 2008 and 2012.

Demand to work for Google is through the roof, which is unsurprising given that, in 2007, Lisa Belkin found that the majority of workers under 30 identify a fun working environment as an important factor in their job search. According to Bloomberg reports, during January 2011, Google received a staggering 75,000 job applications during a *single week*, so the company gets the crème de la crème when it comes to talent. And that talent is earning Google a lot of money – in 2011, when many companies were struggling to stay in business, Google made a profit of almost $10 billion. No wonder they can afford to give away free gourmet food!

Most organizations don't have the luxury of being able to offer gourmet food cooked by world-class chefs, but that doesn't mean that they can't still create a positive working environment, even on a limited budget.

For example, do you recall Innocent, the company we looked at in Chapter G: 'Guiding Values'? In line with being 'generous' with rewards and feedback, Innocent has a Lord or Lady of the Month competition, whereby people get nominated, then recognized for an outstanding contribution, such as going the extra mile to help out teammates or doing really good work. The winner is given a sash and a top hat if they are male or a tiara if they are female, and the rest of the company get down on their knees and pledge allegiance to the Lord or Lady, promising to give them extra special treatment such as making them cups of tea. It's designed to be a bit of fun, with a serious side of recognizing people's contributions.

And fans of *Star Wars* may be inspired to learn that my sister, Jacqueline, is currently delighted to be sitting next to Yoda! Each month her company gives the 'Yoda Award' for the wisest idea with the biggest impact, and the coveted soft toy is passed on to a new winner each month.

 Identify other ways that leaders can introduce fun into their organizational environments – draw upon your own ideas and experience, plus ask friends, family members and colleagues to give you ideas. And have fun implementing them!

 Science has now proved a link between a positive mood and greater productivity. If leaders want their people to achieve more, they should think about how they can create a greater spirit of joy in their working environments.

K: Keep Stakeholders Onside

Keep your friends close, and your enemies closer.
– Sun Tzu

Employees are just one group of people that leaders need to keep happy – other stakeholder groups may include customers, business partners, investors, governing bodies and the local community. In a nutshell, a stakeholder is a person, group or organization who can affect, or is affected by, your operations.

Research shows that relationships with their stakeholders should matter to leaders. For example, in 2002, Paul Nutt analysed 400 strategic decisions and found that *half* of the decisions failed (i.e. were not implemented or led to poor outcomes) because decision makers neglected to attend to the interests and information held by key stakeholders. You will likely be able to think of numerous examples where you've seen or heard of stakeholders becoming hostile and disrupting operations, whether through customer boycotts, local community protests or leadership coups.

Since stakeholders have both the ability to support you to achieve optimum results and also the capacity to hinder your operations, this chapter looks at how you can build and maintain positive relationships with them.

CASE STUDY

At the start of this book, we talked about the moments in time that sparked great visions, such as Gandhi's life-changing train journey and Walt Disney's park bench dream. You may smile when you hear that the idea for one of the world's greatest sporting events, the London Marathon, originated in a pub!

In 1978, two former Olympic runners, John Disley and Chris Brasher, sat in the Dysart Arms, Richmond, a favourite haunt of the Ranelagh Harriers running club, and listened to fellow club members raving about the New York Marathon. Their friends couldn't stop enthusing about how amazing the atmosphere was compared to UK marathons, which at the time were held in country lanes with few competitors and more cows than spectators.

Intrigued by all the fuss, John and Chris decided to enter the 1979 New York Marathon and experience it for themselves. By the end of the race, they had been inspired by its potential, so Chris, who was a sports editor at the *Observer* newspaper, wrote a thought-provoking article about the uniting power of sport:

Last Sunday, in one of the most trouble-stricken cities in the world, 11,532 men and women from forty countries, assisted by over a million people, laughed and cheered and suffered during the greatest folk festival the world has seen. I wonder whether London could stage such a festival … do we have the heart and the hospitality to welcome the world?

Securing stakeholder backing for the first London Marathon was never going to be easy. For a start, John and Chris knew that the police could be highly resistant to the deliberate attempt to draw a large crowd of people together – against a backdrop of recent riots that had occurred in the UK, this would just be asking for trouble. Add to that the need to obtain consent from a wealth of bodies who would be impacted by the race – the local borough councils, the Royal Parks and even the Queen, who would need to authorize the Changing of the Guards to take place earlier!

Yet these two determined individuals succeeded in achieving their vision, and on 29 March 1981, just seventeen months after Chris's article going to print, the first London Marathon took place. Here are five helpful lessons to be learnt from John Disley and Chris Brasher's approach to managing stakeholders.

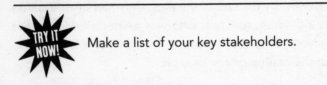 Make a list of your key stakeholders.

1. Build personal relationships with stakeholders at an early stage

Meeting people face-to-face, even just once, really helps to pave the way for a far stronger working relationship, so leaders are wise to invest their time in personally meeting stakeholders, preferably at an early stage of the relationship. This signals the relationship is important, which helps to build trust. It also helps to break down the perception of 'them' and 'us'.

To kick-start the dream of holding the first London Marathon, Chris enlisted the help of his newspaper editor Donald Trelford, who hosted a lunch for representatives from key stakeholder groups and planted the seed of the idea. The pros and cons of a marathon were discussed and it was agreed that the idea was worth pursuing. This also helped to build a positive relationship with bodies such as the police and the Greater London Council, who could have been very resistant and could have even put a halt to the idea, if excluded until a later stage.

- How good are you at building relationships with your key stakeholders at an early stage of your initiative?

- Have you met all of your key stakeholders face-to-face? If not, consider what opportunities you can use to change this.

---

2. Identify needs and wants at an early stage
Relationships in your personal life work best when there is mutual benefit to both parties. Where people feel that their needs are being neglected, they become disgruntled.

Obviously at some times the amount of benefit may be unbalanced – with one party giving more than the other. For the relationship to be successful the imbalance cannot be too significant or for too long. Just like a see-saw, it's best for both parties if either side can go up in the air and not just one.

The same principle applies to managing stakeholder relationships. It should therefore be a key priority (from an early stage) to understand what matters to your stakeholders and to try to accommodate as many of these as is practical into your design. You need to identify:

- 'Must have' needs (things that are critically important)

- 'Should have' needs (things that are fairly important but not essential)

- 'Could have' needs (things that form the icing on the cake).

John and Chris became aware of two 'must have' needs from their stakeholder groups. Firstly, if the race was to go ahead, it could only cause minimal disruption to the London road transport network. Eventually this need was met through careful planning of the route, which required the closure of just two bridges across the River Thames. The second 'must have' need was that the event should be entirely self-funded – not a penny would be given of tax or rate payers' money. Again Chris and John managed to overcome this challenge through getting the buy-in and generous sponsorship from the company Gillette.

THINK ABOUT IT

What are the 'must have' needs of your stakeholder? How can/do you ensure that these are met?

3. Create ambassadors

It is very effective when a representative from an external partner becomes a champion for your idea – people tend to be more accepting if someone in their own group or organization is already advocating a particular course of action.

One of John and Chris's best decisions was to invite two of London's leading police chiefs to accompany them to the next New York Marathon and see how the police there handled the event. The New York Police also acted as advocates for a city-based marathon and were very helpful and hospitable to the London party. The trip was both educating and reassuring to those involved.

Over time the relationship with the police developed so much that, in a newspaper article the night before the first ever marathon, Chris Brasher singled out a police inspector who was heavily involved in the operation, Peter Smith, as someone who kept his own spirits high. Chris said that whenever his own morale was flagging, Peter picked him up by saying, 'Have faith, Chris, it will happen.' When your stakeholders are inspiring you, you know that they are on board!

THINK ABOUT IT

Who are your most resistant/negative stakeholders? Who would be a good ambassador to champion your cause and how can you involve them more?

---

4. Involve

Involving stakeholders in the decision-making process makes them more likely to genuinely commit to the path forward, rather than simply being told to comply with it. As a result, leaders who consult people for their input typically encounter lower resistance to decisions, as people feel a greater sense of ownership of the outcome.

Remember that the people 'on the ground' often have a more detailed understanding of how things work or pan out than the leader, so their input can often also be very valuable in terms of coming up with good ideas. When involving people it is important that you are seen to take their input on board or explain why suggestions have not been adopted, as failure to do this can have highly detrimental consequences, including demotivation and less willingness to volunteer in future.

You can also involve people in the delivery of a project. For example, the local residents on the marathon route could have been very resistant and obstructive to the idea of 7,000 people trampling past their front door. So the organizers actively welcomed them getting involved, asking them to come out onto the streets of London, not only to cheer the crowd on but to provide much-needed water for the thirsty competitors. It's important to stress the benefits of getting involved with a project to balance out some people's natural cynicism and concerns.

 For each of your stakeholder groups, how can you involve them in decision making/delivery to help them to feel a sense of commitment to your initiative?

5. Maintain regular (enough) communication

Problems often occur when there is a breakdown in communication – for example, a 'could have' need has become a 'must have' need but one party isn't aware of the change in circumstances. This can be a particular issue when working with stakeholders who aren't part of your own organization and therefore are at risk of being left out of the loop.

Keeping communication channels open helps to maintain an accurate common understanding between both stakeholder groups, enables on-going involvement, allows you to articulate/celebrate what has been achieved through the stakeholder relationship and will help to cement the relationship further. For example, the marathon organizers notified every household on the route about the event and how they would be impacted, to at least give people notice to make alternative plans.

The strength of the relationship that had been formed between John, Chris and their stakeholders was summed up in Chris's article on 28 March 1981, just hours before the start of the very first London Marathon:

> We are supposed to be suffocating under the weight of bureaucracy and yet my experience in these past few months is that once an organization – whether it be a commercial company, the Metropolitan Police or the Department of the Environment – make up their minds that the event is going to take place, they cut through bureaucracy with a scalpel and expose the heart of the matter.

The race has grown in size, stature and popularity ever since. Now established among the major events in the sporting calendar, the London Marathon is shown on television in more than 150 countries. If you've ever had the privilege of watching or running this incredible race, raise a toast to the vision and determination of John Disley and Chris Brasher and the five-step process they used to keep stakeholders onside.

 The quality and depth of your relationship with stakeholders is one of the most important factors that will determine whether you succeed or fail. Be sure to identify which relationships you need to develop most and demonstrate that every one is a two-way partnership that you value.

L: Listen (With Intent)

Seek first to understand, then to be understood.
– Stephen Covey

A big decision has been made by the leadership team and it has gone down like a lead balloon. You can picture the scene – disgruntled cafeteria conversations, sulking at desks, people close to tears and frustrated outbursts in meetings.

In normal day-to-day life, but especially in tough times, leaders have to make unpopular decisions – that is part and parcel of their job. However, even if they make the *right* decision, it doesn't automatically follow that people will *like* that decision or buy into it.

People can become very annoyed when they feel that their leaders are up in the warm and cosy ivory tower while they, the people at the coalface, are stuck feeling the pain of decisions inflicted upon them. As events unfold, the work environment can become even more toxic, as the really disgruntled people begin to infect those who are just a little jaded. Productivity plummets as the workforce spend their precious time and energy moaning.

When people feel like that no one is listening to them, it is often due to one of three reasons:

1. Leaders have actually failed to listen.

2. Leaders have listened but haven't done anything about it.

3. Leaders have listened and have taken action, but they haven't communicated it well enough.

In this situation, and indeed in everyday life, leaders need to put on their listening 'HAT':

H: Hear – put yourself in an opportunity where you are listening to your people.
A: Act – take action on what you heard.
T: Tell – communicate that you have taken action or help people to believe you have genuinely done all that you can.

H: Hear
When you hear Richard Branson speak about leadership, he frequently refers to the little notebook he carries around with him in his back pocket. For example, while taking a flight on his airline, he describes how he will use the time to get up and talk to the passengers and crew. If an air stewardess complains that her shoes are uncomfortable, he will note it down with the intention of doing something about it. It isn't good for anyone if the staff are in pain for hours on end. The notebook comes out again when Branson is having a few drinks with his staff and the truth starts to come out along with the additional bottles of wine. Rather than letting this precious information be left with the empty

glasses, the important comments get scribbled down for future reference.

 Set up a place on your smartphone where you can add comments.

Try to note down at least one comment every working day for a week, to get you into the habit of listening.

It is important for leaders to consider the most appropriate forum to allow people to vent their frustrations.

Sometimes, good intentions don't actually work well in practice. For example, one leadership team made all leaders attend a compulsory weekly update, which turned into a weekly compulsory moaning session. Those wishing to indulge in the moaning session found it highly cathartic, however, the people who just wanted to get on with the meeting became more and more wound up that their time was being wasted listening to other people going on and on.

An example of a leader who successfully seized an opportunity to listen was the CEO of a company we were working for. When running a residential training course, we were extremely impressed that the CEO gave up his evening to come to the back-end-of-beyond to attend dinner with his senior management team.

This was a really good opportunity for the CEO to engage with his staff. He had all of his organization's leaders in the same room at the same time, in a relaxed environment where they felt able to open up. People could see that he had made an effort to attend and appreciated the time that he made to engage with them on a personal basis, rotating to join different tables throughout the course of the dinner.

A: Act

It wasn't only the presence of the CEO during dinner that impressed us but his responses to the comments that he heard. We noticed that he struck a good balance of listening and talking but critically, when he did speak, his language was very action focused. He provided on-the-spot decisions and empowered his people to move through their barriers.

As the CEO of an extremely busy organization, he wouldn't have had time to address most people's individual concerns so his behaviour was intently focused on listening, digesting information and wherever possible coming up with an instant solution to allow forward progress. When he encountered an issue that could not be resolved on the spot, he asked the person concerned to email him the following week and committed to giving them some more of his time. We had confidence that he would live up to this promise, partly because of how helpful he had already been to others but also because we knew that he was more likely to have time to solve the meatier issues as he wasn't bogged down with the burden of having to revisit the number of smaller actions that had already been dealt with.

On the evaluation forms for the training course, people repeatedly commented how motivating it had been that the CEO had attended.

T: Tell

In contrast, a leader who listens but then does nothing about what he or she hears can have the opposite effect – total demotivation. We worked with a number of middle managers who were totally demoralized from raising serious issues and feeling like they were being ignored. They were tired of making the same points over and over again and had lost all faith in even bothering to give upwards feedback as they believed that it would simply disappear into a black hole.

When we talked to the leadership team of these demoralized middle managers, it became apparent that they were actually trying really hard to resolve the issues at hand. The middle managers had wrongly assumed that no action was being taken, because the leadership team had failed to *communicate* what they were doing. If you are fighting battles on other people's behalves without them knowing about it, they can be slow to appreciate what you are doing for them.

A more difficult situation arises when you have *heard* the problems people are facing, you have taken all of the *action* that you can, but you know that the only update that you can give will still not be good enough. For example, you've heard that people need more money made available, you've taken action to try to secure financial resources, but there simply are no more cookies in the cookie jar. What then?

When leaders are inflicting pain upon their people, they need them to be united behind their decisions, not questioning why *they* (the leaders) did this to *us* (the people). Leaders need to communicate that they have looked at all of the viable options, have evaluated them in terms of the overall mission and have made the best possible decision.

Sometimes it can help to communicate the possible solutions but not the final decision, and instead let the people themselves choose. For example, consider the difference between being told you will have a 20 per cent pay cut versus 'We need to cut costs in order to avoid job losses, here are the options we think are viable and we genuinely want your input into which solution will work best for you.' In this instance you can see the whole listening 'hat' cycle is beginning again.

Be prepared that you may hear that you are the problem

We previously worked with a senior leadership team who were fed up with the low morale that existed within their division. They requested that a compulsory attitude-training course was held for their approximately 100 staff, so that their employees would learn not to be so negative. Senior management were not on the list of provisional course attendees.

Prior to the training course, we interviewed some of the staff and it became apparent that their low morale was largely attributed to the way that they were being led by senior management. As an example, the staff were being asked to attend another mandatory all-day event, while being double-booked to attend a compulsory briefing *and* respond to urgent senior management requests for information during the day. To top it off, they were reprimanded for using their phones during meetings and for missing appointments to meet the latter two requirements. The more the staff voiced their frustrations, the more negative they were perceived to be and the more frustrated senior management became.

In this situation, although it was a hard message to hear, the senior management team had to take on board that it was their own behaviour that needed to change. To their credit, they swallowed the criticism and began to achieve far better results when they gave praise to the people who remained positive under difficult circumstances and thanked people for feedback on how things could be improved.

 Leaders need to *hear*, *act* and *tell* – and then keep listening. Great leaders never take off their listening hats.

M: Motivate

*Motivation is the fuel necessary to keep
the human engine running.*
– Zig Ziglar

Leading a person who doesn't want to be part of a group can be like trying to make water flow uphill. So if leaders want to bring out the best in their people, they need to identify and tap into their motivations for being there – alternatively known as the WIIFM factor. WIIFM is pronounced 'Wifim' and stands for 'What's in it for me?'

Tapping into the WIIFM factor every day

Leaders can use WIIFM on an everyday basis. Take a meeting or training course for example. One of the first questions that must be answered is 'What's the benefit to you from being here?' If attendees can't see how something is relevant to them, they will quickly switch off or, worse, actively resist the session.

Satisfying the WIIFM factor goes deeper than asking the audience, 'What do you hope to gain from this?' or rattling off a list of pre-prepared benefits. Strong leaders ask that question well *before* they have people sitting in front of them, looking at their watches and wondering when they can get back to doing their real work.

Humans often feel that time and energy are precious commodities. Even if we are being paid to sit in a room (and especially when we are not), leaders need to ensure that we are getting value for our time. We all know how aggravating it is to sit through something that is boring and irrelevant.

Look through your diary for the next month and identify any activities where you are a) leading other people or b) being led by other people. How much value for people's time is being created in each of these activities?

When using a portion of someone else's time, ensure that there is a good reason for it and that they are getting benefit from their involvement. The more you can consult with the people involved, asking them what they need in return for their time, the more likely they are to be on board.

This may seem fairly obvious, but remember that common sense isn't always common practice. All of us will be able to identify with the experience of being forced to sit through something that feels completely pointless. Worse still, if your pointless event is a regular occurrence, such as a monthly team meeting, just think how much time you are wasting and ill-feeling you are creating on a routine basis.

Tapping into WIIFM in the longer term

If sitting through a pointless meeting is annoying, it's far worse to be involved with an organization that doesn't meet an individual's long-term needs. So what are typical motivators that need to be satisfied?

Let's start by analysing motivation in a typical leadership context – the working environment. If you ask the question, 'Why do people work?', the obvious answer is 'To earn money.' However, research has shown that although money is an important factor when *deciding* whether to accept a position or not, once a person is actually *established* in a role, other factors become more important when it comes to motivation.

Given that money doesn't motivate people for very long, leaders might like to consider how differently they would treat people if they weren't being paid! So let's explore why people work for free.

Australian researcher Gil Clary and colleagues, through their research ('Volunteers' Motivations: Findings From a National Survey', *Nonprofit and Voluntary Sector Quarterly*, 1996), identified several key reasons why people volunteer. These include:

- To create social interactions and friendships

- To gain experiences that will benefit their careers

- To increase knowledge and skill levels

- To allow the expression of values that are personally important (e.g. altruism, hedonism, recognition, affiliation, etc.)

- Psychological benefit (e.g. increasing self-esteem, feeling a sense of achievement, etc.).

In relation to a *paid* work post that you have held, which of the above factors resonate with your own reasons for working?

These five factors are often important motivators for both paid *and* unpaid work positions. They also apply equally well to participation in an organization, such as an art society or tennis club. Successful leaders provide opportunities for people to meet these important needs, keeping them motivated in the long term.

Earlier in this book, we explored the unusual working environment at Google. Let's revisit this organization's working practices and look at why they are so powerful at satisfying motivational needs:

Social interactions: The design of the workplace actively promotes social interactions, from micro-kitchens, breakout areas and restaurants at the more typical end of the workplace environment to beach volleyball pitches and even a bowling alley at the other end of the spectrum.

Career experiences: Google offers an unusual perk called the '20 Percent Time' programme. This enables Google's engineers to use up to 20 per cent of their working week to pursue projects or activities that are unrelated to their normal job role. A number of Google's technologies have their origins in 20 Percent Time, including Gmail, Google News and even the Google shuttle buses that bring people to work at the company's headquarters in Mountain View, California. Not only do Google's staff benefit developing their careers, but the activities carried out during 20 Percent Time have also proved very lucrative. For example, 20 Percent Time led to the creation of Google's AdSense, which earned their organization $2.9 billion in the first quarter of 2012 alone – that's over 27 per cent of total revenue!

Knowledge and skills: If the 20 Percent Time programme isn't enough to quench a thirst for learning, employees can also attend Google Talks, a programme that brings speakers from all walks of life to their offices to speak on current affairs. Past guests have ranged from violinist Joshua Bell to US presidential candidates Barack Obama and John McCain, and from neuroscientist David Rock to a Buddhist monk, Matthieu Ricard. And best of all, if you want a taste of Google life, you can watch a selection of these excellent talks on YouTube.

Values: Just to give you a flavour:

- Altruism: If you like to donate to charity, Google will match your contributions, up to $12,000 a year.

- Hedonism: Googlers can take advantage of free beer and dance classes, including 'How to dance at a party'.

- Learning: Reimbursement for college or degree qualifications.

- Security: Benefit programmes and amenities that extend to employees' families, e.g. health care and travel insurance.

Psychological benefit: On the 'employee benefits' page, Google Executive Chairman Eric Schmidt states, 'The goal is to strip away everything that gets in our employees' way.' Efforts are made to take the stress and strain out of daily life, whether this takes the form of an on-site bicycle repair or a payment of $500 of 'baby-bonding bucks' for new parents – an amount deposited in their account expected to go towards services that may help them during their first few months like laundry, cleaning, even gardening services.

With all of these opportunities to satisfy employees' key drivers, it's easy to see what's in it for them!

Brainstorm a list of ideas of how you can help your people to satisfy key motivational needs. You could consider some of the following:

- Social interactions: e.g. team socials.

- Career development: e.g. talk aspiring managers through how you planned the department's annual budget.

- Increase knowledge/skill levels: e.g. inviting guest speakers to your organization.

- Values: e.g. enabling a better work–life balance through allowing people to leave early if they've been having to work overtime.

- Psychological benefit: e.g. offering yoga classes during lunch breaks.

Understand the motivational needs behind your people and use the WIIFM factor to bring out the best in them.

N: No More Negativity!

Culture eats strategy for breakfast.
– Peter Drucker

You're leading a team with low morale – their optimism has faded away, emotions are running high and people are becoming distracted from achieving their objectives. As their leader, you've really listened and have genuinely tried to do all that you can, but your hands are tied. There is realistically *nothing* more that you can do to alleviate people's current situation and things are unlikely to improve for the foreseeable future.

For example, imagine that:

- Your operation is failing as a result of extreme influences that are outside your control.

- You can see that your people are suffering – you aren't enjoying it either.

- A blame culture is rife, criticizing the leadership team for failing to do more.

The above scenario has become all too common in recent years since the financial crisis and collapse of Lehman Brothers. Recessions have taken their toll, and attitudes have changed from optimism to fear of the future.

But it turns out that situations have been going on like this for at least a century ... so rewind the clock, it's now 1915 and you are Antarctic explorer Ernest Shackleton:

- Your quest to cross the Antarctic has failed due to appalling environmental conditions. Your ship has been crushed and sunk without a trace, leaving your crew stranded on the freezing cold ice.

- Your team is experiencing massive physical and mental distress.

- You are at risk of severe criticism for leading the crew into this position.

Who is the enemy?

In a bleak, hostile environment, Shackleton's crew could easily have used their precious time and energy arguing among themselves and blaming their leader. For some reason, humans tend to find it rather cathartic to repeatedly explore the questions of *why* this has happened and *whose fault* it is.

Battling against each other, arguing about who was to blame, may *psychologically* have helped the crew to cope. However, when you fight among yourselves, the enemy exists within the team and ultimately this helps no one.

Shackleton led his crew to realize that they did not have time to stand around bickering. They needed to work together to orchestrate their own rescue, and that involved everyone's efforts being channelled in the same direction rather than against each other.

So, vital to Shackleton's eventual success was his ability to focus his team on their real, common enemy – the ice.

 Think of an example of when two parties in a team (who ultimately want the same thing) fought against each other rather than against the common enemy. What impact did this have on the outcome?

Think of an example of when two parties in a team (who ultimately want the same thing) united against a common goal and channelled their efforts towards it together. What impact did this have on the outcome?

Be seen to take a share of the pain

It's a pretty grim scenario – you've just been forced to abandon your sinking ship and you are going to be condemned to spending months living on an ice pack. To top matters off, there are only eighteen warm reindeer sleeping bags to go around, which means that nine people will be left with an inferior woollen bag.

When this situation happened, rather than allow the senior members of the crew to have preferential treatment, Shackleton and his senior officers were included in the draw as to who would receive which bag.

Despite this gesture of fairness, the crew suspected the ballot had been rigged, as reported by crew member William Bakewell: 'There was some crooked work in the drawing, as Sir Ernest, Mr Wild, Captain Worsley and some of the other officers all drew wool bags. The fine warm fur bags all went to the men under them.'

What is the impact on morale when people see the leader being first up to take their share of the pain in a difficult situation?

Shackleton was also very aware of how low morale could spread within the team. He therefore chose to sleep in the same tent as those about whose temperament he was most concerned so as to spare the other crew members from potential disheartening talk, which also had the added benefit of giving attention to those in need. Critically, he did not air these fears about some of the crew aloud to the rest.

People are like batteries – they need recharging or they stop working

You can think of people as batteries – when we are placed in stressful conditions, our batteries are drained of energy. If this continues for too long, we will eventually give up. There is no more that we can give.

Leaders need to be aware of the 'battery levels' of their people and charge them up wherever possible. Shackleton knew that day after day of gruelling pain and suffering would not inspire his crew to keep going. He appreciated that alongside the bad times there had to be some good times to keep spirits high. He therefore encouraged his team to find some pleasure amid the hardship, for example by holding nightly sing-alongs and the odd game of football on the ice. Whenever he noticed his crew were in want of food or drink he encouraged all men to take part in the refreshment, not wanting to single any person out as being more in need than the others.

Fun recharges the batteries

Great leaders are able to create a sense of fun within the team, enabling their people to enjoy the experience of work. For example, we've worked with team leaders who described the challenge of managing large numbers of volunteers doing extremely boring jobs, in potentially grim weather conditions, without being paid. Despite these odds, we've been inspired by the stories of what a fantastic time people can have in this type of situation.

The key to success is the leaders' ability to create a sense of camaraderie in the team. If people are having a good time (at least some of the time), then they don't mind the 'pain' because overall it will be worth it.

Fit your own oxygen mask first

We've worked with hundreds of employees exploring the positive impact of motivation upon performance, and a very common question asked is, 'How can I motivate other people?'

The fundamental answer to this question relates to the analogy of an oxygen mask. During an emergency briefing on an airplane, passengers are instructed to fit their own oxygen mask before they attempt to help others. You can't help other people when you are struggling yourself. The same is true for motivation. It is almost impossible to motivate people when you are demotivated yourself, so if you want to raise morale, you need to hold up the mirror and work on yourself.

If you've ever been led by a demoralized leader you will know just how demotivating it can be. If your leader doesn't believe that things will improve, it is almost impossible for them to inspire hope in you. When there is no hope left, people don't try any more because there isn't any point. And a self-fulfilling prophecy occurs. You have to get control of your emotions if you want to support others. You'll find additional tips in Chapter V: 'Very Stressed!', which will help you to get control of your own emotions.

Can you afford not to tackle negativity?

While Shackleton's entire crew failed against their original goal (to cross the Antarctic continent), they succeeded in their quest to live. In contrast, another Antarctic explorer,

Robert Scott, succeeded along with his team in their 1910 attempt to reach the South Pole, but they failed to survive the expedition.

Sadly, despite Scott's outstanding achievement to reach the South Pole, his team clearly viewed themselves as failures. A sobering photograph of the crew taken at the pole shows five totally demoralized faces – the team had just found out that they were narrowly beaten to the pole by Roald Amundsen's Norwegian crew. Diary entries show how dejected Scott felt: 'The worst has happened'; 'All the day dreams must go'; 'Great God! This is an awful place.'

All members of Scott's team lived to reach the pole. In contrast, every member of the team died after they reached it. It is sobering to ask the question whether the same team would have lived if they had been first to the pole, given that Amundsen and his team all survived.

 When low morale is causing a culture of *them* and *us*, focus a divided team against a common enemy rather than allowing fighting against each other.

O: Outside Your Comfort Zone

A leader takes people where they want to go. A great leader takes people where they don't necessarily want to go, but ought to be.
– Rosalynn Carter

People often ask the question, 'Why push for change when things are OK as they are?' In other words, life in the comfort zone suits them just fine. This chapter explores why people often prefer to stay in their comfort zone, why it is good to step outside of it and how, as a leader, you can inspire others to want to go there.

Make a list of words that you associate with the concept of your staying *within* your comfort zone.

Make a list of words that you associate with the idea of *leaving* your comfort zone.

In our experience, there is often a pattern to the output of this exercise. Words that are associated with staying in the comfort zone are often *positive*, for example, 'easy', 'safe', 'relaxed'. Conversely, words associated with leaving the comfort zone are often *negative*, e.g. 'unpleasant', 'stressful', 'hard work', 'risky'. Given this association, it's easy to see why some people want to keep things just the way they are. If there were a traffic light which signalled red: 'stop' in the comfort zone or green: 'go' outside it, it would be stuck on red!

Why can't I just stay where I am?

Imagine that your comfort zone is represented by a circle. When you step outside of your comfort zone a few times, the size of the circle expands. You get used to doing things that you couldn't previously do and capabilities that were once outside your comfort zone become consumed into it. You can then expand your comfort zone further by taking another step outside of it and repeat this process until your comfort zone becomes really large.

THINK ABOUT IT Imagine that two people have identically sized comfort zone circles. Person A regularly steps outside of their comfort zone and it grows. In contrast, person B stays inside their comfort zone and the circle stays the same size. After a time, what has happened to the size of person B's circle compared to the size of person A's?

When you stay inside of your comfort zone, while others grow around you, the relative size of your comfort zone is actually *shrinking*. To make matters worse, if circumstances change and you *have* to leave your comfort zone when you aren't used to this, it can be much harder to do it, because you aren't used to pushing the boundaries. Contrast this situation with someone who regularly takes steps, big or small, to leave their comfort zone. Their capability expands and they are more likely to feel confident in the face of forced change.

From personal to organizational comfort zones

A UK company had a good market share, a positive reputation and a well-defined product offering, but the organization was failing to innovate beyond its current operational practices. On the face of it, this didn't seem like too much of a problem – profit levels were reasonable and the company had a good track record.

However, the culture was heavily skewed towards maintaining the status quo and, as a result, decision making was very slow. Proposed changes were often reviewed over and over again to make sure they were definitely right, no one wanted to sign their name to proposed changes, and when they were agreed, there was often poor follow-through. Linking back to the word association exercise above, change was seen as *unpleasant*, *stressful*, *hard work* and *risky*.

In contrast, a number of new start-up businesses had entered the organization's market place. These new companies were used to growing rapidly and weren't held back by the bureaucracy that large organizations can face. They were proving that they had the ability to adapt far more quickly to changes in market conditions and were beginning to win new business. They were constantly stepping outside of their comfort zones and they were increasingly proving a real threat to the established organization.

The established organization could no longer afford to be complacent – the CEO sent a clear message to his people in the organization: if they did not change and become better at pushing the boundaries into new territory, the business could lose out to its new competition and, worse still, the business could fail. After a significant amount of work to reshape the culture of the organization, the culture is now very different and the company is much more profitable.

Pushing the boundaries requires leaving the comfort zone

Visionary leaders appreciate that to achieve your potential you have to leave your comfort zone. Henry Ford wanted to push the boundaries and create an assembly line to revolutionize the automobile manufacturing industry. The then Crown Prince of Dubai, Sheikh Mohammed, led his people outside of their comfort zones in creating a palm tree-shaped artificial island. Neither of these aspirations, nor many other leadership visions, could have been achieved without leaders pushing themselves and their people out of their comfort zones.

So how do you get people to *want* to do things that are unpleasant, stressful, hard work and risky?

Is leaving the comfort zone really so bad?

When we run the word association game detailed at the start of the chapter, occasionally there is a different side to the output. People sometimes describe their comfort zone as 'boring', 'stagnant' or 'unfulfilling' and working outside their comfort zone as 'rewarding', 'challenging' and 'exciting'. In other words, their positive and negative associations are reversed – staying in the comfort zone has now become bad and leaving it is good. The traffic light described above changes from red to green – they want to go outside of their comfort zone.

Pain versus pleasure

Humans are driven by a desire to minimize pain and maximize pleasure. It makes evolutionary sense – let's avoid getting ill/cold/injured (pain) and aim to feel warm/full/safe (pleasure).

Whereas at first glance, people may see leaving their comfort zone as *painful*, and staying within it as *pleasurable*, leaders need to help people to change their associations from 'pleasure if we don't, pain if we do' to 'pain if we don't, pleasure if we do'.

For example, the CEO of the company described above needed to switch the association with staying in their comfort zone from good to bad, hence his communication: 'If we don't change, the business could fail.' He then needed to contrast this with a message with stressing the benefits of change – 'pleasure if we do' – more jobs, better bonuses, improved job security, etc.

Linking back to Chapter C: 'Compelling communication', we described how the speeches of Martin Luther King and John F. Kennedy both:

- Referenced the negative consequences of failing to achieve the vision

- Outlined a positive view of the future, should the vision be attempted/realized.

This is also tapping into the message 'pain if we don't, pleasure if we do'.

 With regard to a goal that you would like to achieve, write a list of benefits associated with leaving your comfort zone and positive outcomes from achieving your goal. Then write a list of negative consequences associated with failing to do this.

Think about the ways that you can get this message across to people.

To help you explore this further, we've packed the next chapter with ideas on how leaders can shepherd their people through stages of change.

IF YOU REMEMBER ONE THING Leaders often need to entice people from their comfort zones. If people are struggling to leave, find out what associations they have with staying versus leaving their comfort zones and aim to change the association from 'pain if I do, pleasure if I don't' to 'pain if I don't, pleasure if I do'. In the words of John Maxwell, 'If we're growing, we're always going to be out of our comfort zone.'

P: Progressing Change

*Leadership is the art of getting someone else to do
something you want done because he wants to do it.*
– Dwight D. Eisenhower

Leadership often involves leading people through change.
However, no matter how brilliant an idea for change is, if
people resist it, it will be fruitless. Therefore this chapter
looks at how leaders can inspire others to buy into and progress the change, based on the 'Stages of Change Model'
by Carlo C. DiClemente and James O. Prochaska and the
case study of the 'school dinner revolution' led by celebrity
chef Jamie Oliver.

Stage one: Pre-contemplation

Jamie Oliver felt deep concern about the unhealthy diets of
many British children and embarked upon a personal quest
in 2004 to make school dinners healthier. When Jamie first
started working with the children, they were in the pre-
contemplation stage, which meant they had no intention of
changing their diets – when he tried, it led to mass student
rebellion. Often people stuck in this stage are unaware that
their attitudes or behaviours are problematic, and therefore
their lack of desire to change can be linked to ignorance.

THINK ABOUT IT

Identify a change that you would like to lead but where the people concerned are still in the pre-contemplation phase. Use this example throughout the chapter to explore how you can bring about this change.

Stage two: Contemplation

During a change initiative, the leader often needs to open up people's minds to the fact that change is needed. You may have heard the saying that 'You don't know what you don't know' – so raising awareness is key.

In a rather unpleasant piece of television footage, Jamie Oliver asks a group of school children whether they would rather eat chicken nuggets and chips or chicken meat and vegetables. You can imagine where the unanimous vote fell! So Jamie then proceeds to explain how chicken nuggets are made. He pulverizes a chicken carcass and chicken skin in a food processor and mixes it with breadcrumbs. It is enough to put anyone off eating chicken nuggets for life!

The British government has also successfully used shock tactics for many years to raise awareness of serious issues, such as the need to wear a seatbelt or fit a smoke alarm. Often these campaigns are quite brutal – at the time of writing, a new campaign was launched showing sobering footage of people falling onto railway lines and experiencing hair-raising near misses with trains. This campaign has a mixture of emotion (shocking footage) combined with logic (in the form of statistics about accidents narrated over the footage). It demonstrates that awareness for change can be raised through stirring people's emotion, appealing to people's logic, or a combination of the two.

Although negative emotional messages can be very powerful, when you use them you must avoid creating unnecessary panic. A campaign that shocks people into fitting a smoke alarm is positive, but something that makes children cry at night for fear of their house burning down is bad.

Remember that you have the power to use both the stick (negative emotional tactics, which shock people into change) and the carrot (positive emotional tactics, which promote the benefits of change). A leader's job is to select the best method for raising awareness and select the appropriate audience and timing for that message.

When raising awareness for the need for change, leaders may find it useful to structure their message using the marketing principle AIDA:

A: Attention – find a way to grab people's attention.
I: Interest – increase interest by outlining compelling advantages and benefits.
D: Desire – communicate how taking action will satisfy people's needs.
A: Action – give a clear and powerful call to action of the first step to take towards change.

THINK ABOUT IT

How did/could Jamie Oliver have used the AIDA principle to raise awareness of healthy eating?

How could you use AIDA to help raise awareness of the need to change in your example (as identified in the previous 'Think about it' exercise on page 126)?

Stage three – Action

In this stage, people deliberately change their former actions in favour of new desirable behaviours. It can often be very painful implementing a change, both for those on the receiving end and also for those driving it. Here are some tips for successfully navigating this stage, summed up with this ACTION acronym.

A: Advocates

Ensure that the people who will be initiating the change on your behalf are on your side. For example, Jamie Oliver spent time winning over the dinner ladies at his pilot school who would deliver the change. Implementing the change involved effort and stress, and the initiative would have failed if disgruntled staff had walked out. Jamie won staff over by displaying passion and belief in the cause and through getting his hands dirty too, offering his personal phone number to the dinner ladies who could call when they needed support.

C: Copying behaviour

Some people are naturally more open to change than others. Find these early adopters and make them visible. Once a few people have started to change, others will be more likely to follow. For example, it was fascinating to watch footage demonstrating how the school children copied each other's eating behaviours – if some people are seen to enjoy healthy food, others will start trying it too. Jamie also used this tactic with the staff. Initially he worked with just one school and proved that a new healthy eating regime could work. He then took the initiative to other schools in the borough of Greenwich, who bought into it because there was proof from the first school that the vision could become realized.

T: Thank you

It is important to reward people for trying new behaviours. The school children responded well to praise and thrived on receiving sticker rewards for their efforts! While handing out gold sticky stars might not be quite the done thing in an office, think about how motivating they were when you were a child. Reflect upon how powerful it is when leaders take time to give personal recognition both to those involved in the change and those managing it.

I: Involvement

You can increase buy-in by getting people involved with the change, so that they become active contributors rather than just passive recipients. Jamie Oliver experienced great success from allowing the kids to cook their own food, making them much more likely to try something different, and the children also benefitted from the introduction of 'food weeks' where they learnt about food in every class subject.

O: OK to implement

Change is often resisted because breaking with the norm involves extra effort and pain. The school dinner ladies clearly suffered in terms of extra stress and extra hours in order to implement the new food regime. Leaders need to do whatever they can to make the implementation of change easier. For example, Jamie provided a 'school dinner bible' for every school, with recipes clearly laid out and tips for good kitchen practice.

N: New skills and equipment

Leaders need to be aware that change initiatives may need to be supported by new skills and equipment in order to get the change up and running. During the initial phase of implementation, extra resources may need to be brought in to support people as they get up to speed. For example, the dinner ladies required training how to cook the new food, new equipment to cook with and some benefitted from temporary support from army chefs that were brought in as the programme was initiated.

THINK ABOUT IT

How could you apply the ACTION principles to the change that you would like to implement?

Stage four – Maintenance

Implementing the change is one thing, sustaining it is another, so what can leaders do to encourage long-term adoption of the change?

Eliminate access to old ways to avoid temptation of slipping back

Jamie was convinced that to maintain the healthy eating regime, it was important to take junk food off the menu permanently. With enticing burgers and chips, compared with chicken thigh and broccoli, you can see why there was concern that, given the choice, kids would slip back into old ways.

Financial investment needs to be sustained

During a change process, money is often thrown at launching the change. However, for the benefits of that investment to be realized, funding will likely need to continue and be actively managed throughout the duration of the project.

Jamie Oliver had created a healthy school dinners regime in the borough of Greenwich that was successfully working – over 10,000 students in 27 schools were being served with the new style of school dinners; however, Jamie accepted that there was a key issue surrounding dinner lady pay. The new food was clearly taking much longer to prepare and the dinner ladies were becoming understandably disgruntled for having to work extra hours without additional compensation. For the change to be sustained, it would be necessary to increase funding.

Before going to sponsors with a begging bowl, leaders can help themselves by asking whether they have done everything that they can to save costs. For example, Jamie negotiated with the wholesalers for price reductions.

Where cost increases are unavoidable, it is much easier to get buy-in from financial sponsors if they can see that they are getting significant benefit for proportionally not a lot more. Do your homework first and go in with a strong business case.

Remember you can use both logical and emotional arguments – it is inspiring to hear parents and teachers enthuse about how much better behaved, calmer and more focused their children were once the sugar highs from junk food had been eliminated. Also there is nothing like creating a bit of empathy to make your point – serving up an unpalatable old style school dinner comprised of reprocessed meat to the Secretary of State for Education certainly made the point well! It helped Jamie to go on and secure £280 million in funding from Prime Minister Tony Blair to improve school food.

Stage five – Termination

According to the Stages of Change model, 'Termination' occurs when the change is so ingrained that it would be unthinkable to return to the old habits.

In 2012, eight years after the initial project began, Jamie Oliver's personal website still has content devoted to the school dinners campaign, with updates of progress for each year since the TV show first aired in 2005. The update for the year 2012 reads, 'The fight continues', so clearly this change initiative is not in its termination phase yet. However, it is inspiring to read what has been achieved so far.

- In 2006, junk food was banned in schools, and new legal food-based standards for school food were brought in and were raised further in 2008. They are now in place across the majority of schools in England and continue to be a legal requirement.

- Following concern that uptake of school dinners was falling as a result of junk food being banned, school meal uptake started to rise again in 2009, a trend which continues.

- Research on the schools in Greenwich has shown a clear link between better school food and lower absenteeism and improvements in results and pupil behaviour. The University of Essex concluded that the healthier eating in Jamie's schools improved pupil grades.

This is probably one of the most important and biggest food revolutions in this country ever.
– Jamie Oliver

 For a change to be successful, leaders need to support their people to move through the five stages of change. A relapse to old ways can occur at any stage, so it is important that the leader supports the change until it is thoroughly embedded. The results of perseverance can be very inspirational.

Q: Qualities for Leadership

Personality is to a man what perfume is to a flower.
– Charles M. Schwab

 What impact does personality have on how leaders are perceived and how effective they are at their jobs?

You carry your personality with you all of the time

Let's imagine that you work in an office. Some people in your team will greet you first thing in the morning and will have a chat: 'I had a really bad journey to work today'; 'Have you seen the new colour of the foyer?'; 'I'm really not looking forward to going to the gym at lunchtime.' Others will come in, say a quick hello and will put their heads down and start working. This behaviour may be exaggerated one way or the other on quiet or busy days; however, it will be a relatively stable trait.

And here's the interesting part. You don't walk into your office in the morning and think, 'Oh, I'm an extrovert, I need to have a chat!' You just act subconsciously.

You take your subconsciously driven behaviour with you

from your desk, to team meetings, to your most important customer-facing moments, to the canteen and more. Your personality is with you *all of the time* and impacts every interaction you have (or choose not to have!).

Personality impacts how we are perceived by others: 'She's really friendly/bossy/organized/bad-tempered/lively/stressed out!' It can also have an impact on how well suited we are to our jobs. While there is no good or bad personality trait per se, there can be personality traits which are better or worse suited to a particular job. Let's imagine that you are recruiting for the position of head of health and safety at a nuclear power plant – broadly speaking, would you want someone in this role who a) respects rules and wants them upheld, or b) who views rules more as 'guidelines' that are there to be broken? If you've watched *The Simpsons*, just think, would you appoint Homer?

 What personality traits do you think typically support effective leadership?

Our research

We asked 40 senior leaders to imagine that they had to recruit someone into their own job role, and they were tasked with trying to identify the very best set of personality characteristics for successful leadership.

We've described the top five personality traits below that our research participants identified as helpful to strong leadership, listed in order of importance. The results suggest that leaders need to be:

Emotionally stable: Leaders take life's events and demands in their stride, demonstrating a calm and mature attitude under pressure. Rather than exhibiting lots of ups and downs, strong leaders say that there is rarely a problem they can't cope with and calmly face both the big and the small things that go wrong in their working and personal lives. *95 per cent of our research participants rated this behaviour as very important to successful leadership.*

Warm and outgoing: Reserved, impersonal, aloof and detached behaviour does not support effective leadership. In contrast, strong leaders are charismatic, affable and friendly and enjoy working with other people. *90 per cent of participants rated this behaviour as very important to successful leadership.*

Socially confident: Leaders need to feel at ease in social situations. It helps if they find it easy to strike up conversations with strangers and can quickly fit into a new group. They feel comfortable being the centre of attention, such as giving presentations or speaking in front of other people. *83 per cent of participants rated this behaviour as very important to successful leadership.*

Role models for following the rules: Cultures where people are expedient and deliberately disregard rules may lead to undesirable behaviour and a loss of control. Therefore leaders need to be the model of the right way to behave – if the leader is regularly breaking the rules, you can't expect anyone else to abide by them. Participants did however comment that leaders may need to *bend* the rules to manage exceptional circumstances, however *discretion* was needed around this, and leaders should generally be perceived to abide by expected policies and procedures. *80 per cent of participants rated this behaviour as very important to successful leadership.*

Able to strike a balance between dominant and accommodating behaviour: Although at first thought, dominance might be perceived as a good trait for leadership, imagine what it would be like to be led by someone who was constantly aggressive, forceful and vocal or critical in expressing their opinions. In contrast, our research participants felt that leaders would flounder if they were docile, deferential and too easily led. Therefore, they concluded that it was appropriate to strike a balance between dominant and co-operative behaviour, generally being seen as consultative and accommodating to people's needs while feeling confident enough to take a much more assertive stance when situations demanded it. *73 per cent of participants rated the behaviour described above as very important to leadership.*

Applying the research to real-life leadership

It's fascinating to explore how these personality traits play out in real-life leadership. Let's look a very famous leader, HM Queen Elizabeth II.

- She is patient, relaxed and incredibly calm under pressure, as demonstrated by her composure in the aftermath of the death of Diana, Princess of Wales.

- Her wealth of experience as a monarch has led to her developing sound social confidence – she is described as being gifted at helping people to feel at ease in her company.

- She displays the utmost integrity at all times and is exemplary when it comes to upholding rules and protocols.

- Despite being Head of State, and therefore holding a very powerful position, she is renowned for being highly diplomatic, seeking consensus and taking advice.

Despite her sound leadership, the Queen has been criticized in the past by the British press for displaying a lack of warmth – the second most important personality trait in our research. However, more recently the press describe that the Queen has modified her behaviour away from a detached and formal approach, towards a warmer demeanour. Interestingly, this shift in behaviour has correlated with an increase in her popularity in recent times.

TRY IT NOW! For each of the five behaviours above where do you feel that you have a natural fit?

For areas where you do have a natural fit, you are likely to be able to just be yourself and you will get good results. But what about the sub-optimal areas?

TRY IT NOW! Pick up a pen and sign your name. How does that feel?

Now swap the pen to your other hand and sign your name again. How does it feel this time?

People typically say that they find it natural and effortless to sign their name with their normal writing hand. In contrast, they have to concentrate harder when writing with their non-dominant hand – they can do it, but the results aren't typically as good and it gets tiring after a while.

The same is true for personality. If you know that it's good to keep calm under pressure, but that isn't your natural temperament, if you try really hard, it is possible to keep emotional control. You may not be able to do it quite as well as a naturally calmer person, however, you can get better results than if you didn't try at all. So the key to modifying your behaviour is to become conscious about the things that help and hinder your personality, and to consciously aim to modify the areas that hold you back.

- Make a list of personality traits that you have that positively support leadership.

- Make a list of personality traits that you have that undermine your effectiveness as a leader.

Although personality is a relatively stable trait, over time, it is possible to mould aspects of your personality so you feel more natural acting in a certain desirable way. It's just like writing with your non-dominant hand for six months – if you persist long enough, you will get better. For example, you can learn to get more confident being the centre of attention, or learn to step back and let others speak before making a decision. The trick is to be consciously aware of how you want to behave and put effort into bringing this to life.

Too much of a good thing

We've looked at aspects of personality that are typically seen to be desirable for leadership, however, leaders should be careful of the downsides of their strengths and make sure they aren't over-using them.

Research, linked to the creation of a psychometric test called the Hogan Development Survey, has found that certain personality traits are helpful to leaders, but over-use can lead to their downfall.

For example, let's take someone who is self-confident. A healthy amount of self-confidence is positive when leading others. However, having *too much* self-confidence can lead to arrogance and a tendency to think that you are so good you don't need any feedback. As you'll see in Chapter X: 'eXit', where leaders arrogantly ignore helpful suggestions for improvement, they can face long-term failure, becoming out of touch with reality.

Looking at another example, being diligent can be very positive – someone who is organized, hardworking and attends to detail can get good results from their work. However, if they become overly perfectionist, people can find them hard to work with. Just think of someone like Steve Jobs, former CEO of Apple. His strength lay in his desire for exceptional standards, such as beautiful design; however, he admitted himself the downside of this, giving a perception of being fussy, critical and stubborn, which sometimes reflected poorly on him.

 For the areas of your personality that you feel positively assist your leadership capability, reflect on whether you ever over-use these traits. If you do, be mindful to rein these in, as well as focusing on developing weaker areas.

 You carry your personality around all of the time. Start being conscious of where your personality brings out the best and the worst in people and situations and aim to modify your behaviour to create optimum results.

R: Respect and Integrity

The supreme quality for a leader is unquestionably
integrity. Without it no real success is possible.
– Dwight D. Eisenhower

Imagine that you are erecting a large canvas tent. The tent has four corner poles and an additional centre pole. As you build the tent, it becomes clear that the purpose of each corner pole is to increase the volume of the tent – if a corner pole is missing the tent can still stand, there will simply be less space inside. In contrast, the centre pole is critical – without this being securely in place, the tent is likely to collapse.

Building on this concept, researchers John Zenger and Joseph Folkman have created a great metaphor called 'The Leadership Tent'. In their tent analogy:

- The space underneath the canvas represents the leader's overall capability – the more space, the better the leader

- Each corner pole represents a cluster of related skills (e.g. strong leadership during times of change), which helps the leader to succeed

- The centre pole represents the leader's character.

In the analogy, while putting up a corner pole is highly desirable, a leader *can* survive with weaker performance in these areas. However, Zenger and Folkman's research concluded that the centre pole of character is absolutely *critical* to leadership.

> '*A person who receives low marks on character has absolutely no chance of being perceived as a great leader, especially in the long run.*'
> – John Zenger & Joseph Folkman
> (*The Handbook for Leaders*, 2004)

Negative character traits include:

- 'Smiling up whilst kicking down'
- Failing to create a lack of trust, for example by reneging on promises made
- Acting immorally
- Putting personal agenda ahead of what is right for the organization
- Saying one thing and doing another.

 What other behaviours would you consider to be negative character traits?

How much would you like to be led by someone who has these character traits?

The impact of a weak centre pole

At the time of writing, Great Britain is undergoing a major political and media crisis, nicknamed 'The Phone Hacking Scandal'. Although the public inquiry concerning possible malpractice is yet to be concluded, allegations have included instances of police bribery and journalists hacking into the voicemails of celebrities and crime victims.

It has been eye-opening to watch the impact of these events upon leaders associated with this crisis. Just as Zenger and Folkman's research predicted, once an associated leader's reputation had been dented (rightly or wrongly) they were forced to resign. This included a number of high-profile leaders from the newspaper at the centre of the scandal, the *News of the World*. Allegations of malpractice didn't only bring down the newspaper's leaders but ultimately led to the closure of the entire publication.

And the fallout did not stop there. Events have shown that it is not only a leader's *own* actions that matter, since their reputation can be negatively impacted by those they choose to *associate* with. For example, the reputations of many senior politicians, including the prime minister, have been called into question through their personal and professional relationships with people at the centre of the scandal, despite the fact that they insist they have acted with the upmost integrity at all times. Even in the absence of any wrongdoing, this has been a distraction which they could have done without and has tarnished their own reputations.

How much is your integrity worth?

Once lost, integrity is almost impossible to recover. When a journalist hacks someone's voicemail, they are effectively risking their integrity for the benefit of a possibly sensational story (alternatively known as tomorrow's chip shop paper).

Co-founder of Innocent Richard Reed prides himself on displaying respect and integrity and has spoken about the interesting origin of his value for it. As a teenager, he was caught attempting to steal a cardboard cut-out promotion featuring the model Eva Herzigová from a department store in Huddersfield:

> My dad happened to be walking past, just at the point where I'd been nabbed by the store manager, and I thought I was going to get told off by my dad for trying to steal this thing, and my dad just said to me: 'It's up to you how you price your own integrity. If you want to sell your integrity for a piece of cardboard with a picture of a woman on it, that's your decision but I think that you should pay a higher price than that.'

Richard Reed links the personal value of integrity to tangible business benefits. If you treat people disrespectfully, they stop wanting to work for you. In contrast, if leaders create an organization with genuine integrity that treats people well, they attract the best and brightest minds out there.

THINK ABOUT IT It is worth asking yourself the following sobering question: what have you traded your personal integrity for in the past?

In a world of office politics, it's all too easy to get sucked into a word of gossiping. Employees often spend many hours at work, in a pressure cooker environment, with people that they wouldn't necessarily choose to associate with, and sometimes it feels cathartic to have a good old 'bitch' about a colleague behind their back. But inevitably your comments get back to the person concerned through the grapevine, then people start to raise the question to themselves: 'If they say that about "x", what do they say about me behind my back?'

When you read the analogy of the leadership tent, you realize just how self-destructing this behaviour can be. And if you are the leader, just think of the example you are setting. If you want to lead an organization that fosters a positive culture of trust, where people speak respectfully to and about each other, you need to lead the way through your own behaviour. We'll explore this further in the next chapter.

Commanding respect

So we've talked about the importance of being seen to have integrity, but thinking more broadly than this, how do leaders command respect? A great leader to consider in this situation is HM Queen Elizabeth II.

At the time of writing, the Queen has just celebrated her Diamond Jubilee, marking 60 years on the throne of the United Kingdom. As we listened to her thanking her people for their contributions to the celebrations, we felt a deep sense of pride for our long-serving leader. Aside from the fact that she always acts with unquestionable integrity, in particular it is her dedication to her work that commands our respect.

On the monarchy's official website you can read what it's like in a day in the life of Queen Elizabeth II. Every day the Queen receives 200–300 letters from the public, sometimes more. She reads a selection of letters herself, enabling her to keep in touch with a cross-section of the public (remember the importance of leaders wearing their 'listening hat' in Chapter L: 'Listen') and advises on what reply to make. Almost every letter is responded to personally by a member of her staff.

Every day of every year, wherever she is, the Queen receives policy papers, Cabinet documents, telegrams, letters and other State papers. All of these papers have to be read and, where necessary, approved and signed. She will often spend upwards of an hour reviewing this official correspondence.

After lunch she will often go out and do public engagements, and the Queen prepares personally for each event by reviewing who she will be meeting and what she will be seeing and doing. The Queen may end the day by seeing government ministers, such as the prime minister, or attending further public engagements. All in all, the Queen carries out around 430 engagements a year – an impressive statistic for someone who will soon be 90 years old.

The respect I have for the Queen reminds me of the respect that I had for the former head teacher of my secondary school, Miss Cavendish. If there was a school play, she would attend every night, even when there were three or four performances of the same show. She made an effort to get to know each pupil personally and she treated us fairly against the rules that had been set. Like the Queen, she had an unflappable demeanour; she put us at ease in her presence and she always brought a positive and sensible approach to every situation. Critically, she never asked for our respect, she just had it. When she announced her retirement, staff, pupils and parents alike were very sad that she would be leaving.

 Which leaders do you have immense respect for? What is it about them that commands respect?

Rate yourself, on a scale of 1 (very poor) to 5 (excellent), against the following statements:

- I act with integrity at all times.

- I am dedicated to my work/cause.

- I treat other people respectfully, regardless of their role and position.

- I speak respectfully about other people.

- I am open to feedback and am seen to act upon it.

- I choose to associate with other people who have high integrity.

These are all examples of small behaviours that you can demonstrate which will increase the amount of respect people have for you.

 A leader has zero chance of being perceived a good leader in the long run if his or her character comes into question. Ensure that you act with respect and integrity at all times, as it is of the utmost importance.

S: Set an Example

Be the change that you want to see in the world.
– Mohandas Gandhi

Your behaviour sets the standard

James was an experienced leader and was delighted to be appointed as a senior leader in an overseas organization. After the first couple of weeks of making an effort to dress smartly, like many of us, he had reverted back to his normal work wardrobe. He'd come from a country where dress at work was relatively casual and he didn't think anything of turning up to work in jeans.

After a couple of days of wearing jeans, James's boss, Sean, asked him for a quiet word. Sean was concerned that James's dress code would infect the team beneath him and would lower standards. James's team frequently met external visitors and stakeholders, and, given that he was leading a high-profile project within the organization, it was important that the team created an air of professionalism at every opportunity.

James took the feedback to heart. He got rid of his old wardrobe, which he could now see was well past its best, and, in his own words, 'spent a fortune on suits'. He analysed every aspect of his personal appearance and hygiene: he made a commitment to shave every day, ensure fresh breath at all times, always wear well-ironed shirts and never to have scruffy shoes. And he didn't stop there – James then began to drum the importance of high standards of dress and personal hygiene into his own team. He was determined that his division would have the highest standards in the entire organization. And over time this was achieved. Even people in the lowest levels of the organizational hierarchy underneath James, who had relatively infrequent contact with him, were consistently impeccably dressed, and the standards in James's division became noticeably higher than other teams.

We recently had the privilege of meeting James's daughter, who was visiting her father and wanted some advice regarding her future career. Knowing the backstory of James's dress code experience, we smiled as she walked into the coffee bar – she was immaculately dressed from head to toe and made a very positive impression. A business leader's example extends well beyond the office doors.

THINK ABOUT IT

- Who do you set an example to in your life and career?

- What example would you like to set?

- Where are you achieving this and where can you raise the bar?

Say and do the same thing

James achieved results because he said and did the same thing – so what happens when there is a mismatch between what you see and hear? Imagine that you worked in the following organization and experienced this real-life scenario.

It's 2008, and your company is suffering as a result of the economic recession. Bizarrely, you've just been notified that there will be a blanket ban on company-funded biscuits in internal meetings. This has caused a sense of outrage among your peers – what a petty management decision … biscuits really don't cost that much.

Word quickly gets round that this is designed to be a subtle message that economic conditions are biting and that redundancies are likely. In other words, the biscuit ban is designed to psychologically prepare people for change.

In keeping with the subtle message of the biscuit ban, you keep hearing the senior management team talking about the need for austerity: 'Everyone has to do their bit, even down to forgoing biscuits in their meetings.'

So imagine how you would feel if one day, sitting in the canteen at lunchtime, you look out of the window at the directors' car park and see a plush new set of company cars being delivered for the senior management team. How comfortably would the 'Everyone needs to do their bit' message sit with you?

- Ask a group of people to hold their hand in front of themselves and make a 'beak' by touching their thumb with their index finger.

- Ask them to begin tweaking their beak (i.e. pincering your thumb and index finger together) and do this action yourself at the same time.

- As they are tweaking, clearly say, 'Place your beak against your chin' but, as you say this, place your own beak against your cheek.

- Look to see how many people have their beak against their cheek rather than their chin.

We have run a version of this exercise in many leadership development training sessions and always see examples of people following what they *see* rather than what they're told to do.

As leaders, it is important to remember that it isn't only *what* you say that is important. Next time you communicate, make sure that your behaviour is consistent with the message that you are trying to promote.

Create a set of behavioural commandments for you to follow.

Write a list of ten things that you commit to doing or not doing when working with your team and other people in the organization. For example:

- 'I will be on time for meetings.'

- 'I won't constantly check my phone when I'm meant to be listening.'

- 'I will arrive at work well presented.'

- 'I will say hello to people when I walk into the office in the morning.'

Never underestimate the impact setting an example can have

When Princess Diana sadly died in 1997 almost half of the world watched her funeral. The 'People's Princess', as she was popularly called, had been named in *Time* magazine's '100 Most Important People of the 20th Century', yet she was no political leader, ruler of a country or business leader. Instead, she had something she was passionate about that she dedicated her energy to: humankind.

Princess Diana devoted her time to bring awareness to those suffering from any number of conditions, whether it was hunger, leprosy or loss of life from landmines. Perhaps former US President Bill Clinton summed it up best:

In 1987, when so many still believed that AIDS could be contracted through casual contact, Princess Diana sat on the sickbed of a man with AIDS and held his hand. She showed the world that people with AIDS deserve not isolation, but compassion. It helped change world opinion, helped give hope to people with AIDS, and helped save lives of people at risk.

Princess Diana showed by her actions that she valued everybody, regardless of status or condition. By doing so she helped change people's opinions for the better, through just the use of her time and her compassion.

The darkest hour is the most important time to show the way

A crisis has a way of revealing the leader for who they truly are. At these moments, all eyes may be on you for the example you set. And where the crisis is unexpected, you will have no time to prepare or compose yourself. You simply must lead, and lead well.

This was what Rudy Giuliani faced on the day of Tuesday 11 September 2001, forever remembered as 9/11 and the day the Twin Towers of New York were attacked by terrorists. Rudy was finishing breakfast when he heard that a plane had hit the North Tower. He went straight to the World Trade Center and watched the events unfold in person.

While he may have been the city's elected leader, that day he was also the emotional leader. With a city facing panic and anger he remained focused, working with the fire commissioner and police commissioner to help them get what they needed. Giuliani was able to phone the local TV broadcaster NY1 and asked for people to remain calm but to evacuate from Lower Manhattan. Hours later he was beside Governor George Pataki, giving a press conference. With the eyes of millions of Americans on him he spoke softly, repeating the need for calm in the face of what had happened. He also offered New Yorkers hope at a frightening time, urging them to be resilient and focus on being united:

> Tomorrow, New York is going to be here. And we're going to rebuild, and we're going to be stronger than we were before. I want the people of New York to be an example to the rest of the country, and the rest of the world, that terrorism can't stop us.

Even after the crisis was over, Giuliani set the example of how to mourn those that had been taken away in such shocking circumstances. Giuliani attended up to five funerals a day for those who had died on 9/11, including those in the emergency services who had acted so bravely to save those trapped in the towers, always leading the mourners in giving the departed a standing ovation.

IF YOU REMEMBER ONE THING Leaders are role models and, as a result, their behaviour can bring out the best and the worst in their people. If you don't like the behaviour you're seeing, or you want to shape the attitude and actions of others, look first to your own actions and be the change you want to see.

T: Times Change

The philosophy of the schoolroom in one generation will
be the philosophy of government in the next.
– Abraham Lincoln

Most of us will be familiar with the concept of an office vending machine, stuffed with crisps and sweets, for when we really need that chocolate fix; however, if you work for Facebook, the vending machine contains computer equipment! If you need a new keyboard or mouse, you don't need to wait for the IT team to turn up, you can just go and get one right out of the vending machine. The world of work is changing.

My grandfather worked for an electronics company. He cycled to his office, worked set 9–5 hours, came home for lunch every day and completed more than 30 years of service for the same organization. During his career, letters and documents were typed up by ladies working in the typing pool, with a typical turnaround time of a week.

My father worked as an electrical engineer. He had a long commute, worked crazy hours and was employed by a handful of companies. During his career, computers became mainstream and faxes were superseded by emails.

And the world of work continues to evolve. For example, our business's first piece of client work involved writing a 30-module training programme for an American author, based upon her book. We met through an internet business site and she chose to conduct the relationship entirely by email, so we never spoke to her and we had no idea what she looked like (OK, so we admit we did take a sneaky look at a picture on the internet!).

As technology continues to evolve and new generations enter the workforce, leaders need to keep up with the changes and adapt their working cultures appropriately.

Generation Y

'Generation Y' or 'Gen Y' is the name given to people born roughly between the late 1970s and early 1990s. Although Gen Y is clearly a stereotype to which not everyone conforms, it is interesting to explore the typical characteristics of this generation, since it now forms a significant chunk of the working population who will eventually lead and manage the next generation.

Gen Y watched their parents, known as 'Baby Boomers', slave away in the long-hours culture of the 1980s and 1990s. Put off by having witnessed the downsides of working all hours, members of Gen Y often want to 'work to live', not 'live to work'. According to a study called 'No Collar Works' by MTV, 89 per cent of Gen Y want their workplace to be social and fun (compared to only 60 per cent of Baby Boomers); 81 per cent think they should be allowed to make their own hours at work (compared to only 69 per cent of Baby Boomers) and 75 per cent would like to work for themselves one day, reflecting their belief that if you work hard you should be rewarded for it.

Gen Y have grown up with technology playing a major part in their lives – in December 2011, the *Daily Mail* newspaper reported that over 1 million British eighteen-year-olds are registered on Facebook, compared to only 520,000 on the electoral role – in other words twice as many people can use Facebook than vote! In a world of internet-enabled smartphones, it is difficult to stop people checking Facebook, Twitter and personal email throughout the working day. Moreover, many young people find it unreasonable to be denied access to social networking during working hours – their employers often expect them to work outside of normal office hours, so it is only fair to have a little give and take.

Gen Y's parents have also been nicknamed as 'helicopter parents' who lavish their children with praise and pay close attention to their children's experiences and problems. The term 'helicopter' relates to the fact that help is rarely far away and, as a result, many members of Gen Y have grown up expecting help to be given when requested. In Scandinavia, the term 'curling parenthood' is also used, which describes parents' attempts to sweep all obstacles out of the paths of their children.

Some more stats from the MTV survey shed further light on the mindset of Gen Y:

- 92 per cent think their company is lucky to have them as an employee.

- 80 per cent think they deserve to be recognized more for their work.

- Over half want feedback at least once a week or more, while only 6 per cent prefer annual reviews from their bosses.

- 89 per cent think it is important to be constantly learning at their job.

- 90 per cent think they deserve their dream job.

- Only one quarter say they are completely satisfied in their current job (half the level of the Baby Boomers).

What is the traditional organizational mindset when it comes to:

- When people are expected to work?

- Where people are expected to work?

- The way people spend their time when they are at work?

- How people are rewarded?

- How people receive feedback?

- The factors that enable people to be promoted?

- Requests for flexible working, e.g. flexible hours, working part-time or taking sabbaticals?

- The facilities/services people expect at work?

How could leaders adapt the working culture to play to the strengths and values of Gen Y and why would they benefit from this?

It's time to do some very different thinking

I recently received a speculative email from a recruitment consultant who found my profile on the business-networking site LinkedIn (note the new world of recruitment!). He had a vacancy for a job at an 'extremely cutting-edge firm' and he wondered if I would be interested.

As someone just about scraping into the upper end of Gen Y, two things are very important to me. Firstly, the ability to work flexible hours and, secondly, the ability to work from home on a regular basis ... that is why I chose to become self-employed. The only question I asked the recruiter was: 'Would the hiring company be interested in working with someone on a basis other than a full-time office-based employee?' The answer was a flat 'no'. When I put the phone down, I asked myself, just how 'cutting-edge' is this firm then? It was a real shame because I would have enjoyed working in partnership with the organization concerned and thought that their work could have dove-tailed well with my skill set. But the mindset of how organizations operate (or perhaps how recruitment consultants are paid) was still too fixed to have even asked the question 'Could this partnership work?'

There is a conception that work involves going to a place of work, for set hours, doing a set type of work, often with the same people. Work is done in a certain way, for example, we attend team meetings on a monthly basis and update our colleagues on what we have done and aspects that are forthcoming. But just because that is the way that it has *always* been done, doesn't mean that it is the *only* or *best* way. As the new generation moves into the workforce, leaders need to adapt the culture to ensure that they bring out the best in a demanding generation.

Support the generations to collide

I volunteer on the committee of the 'old girls' association at my school. Each year the committee team organizes a lunch for people wishing to visit the school and meet up with old friends. It is fair to say that I am always by far the youngest person at the event, as exemplified by this year's activity for the 'old girls' to recall their memories of the London Olympics in 1948!

The event is very poorly attended by anyone below the age of about 60, and as the youngest 'old girl' committee member, people often ask me, how can we make the event more enticing for the younger generation? After all, over time, the older generation will no longer be able to come, and we risk the event fizzling out.

I dutifully began beavering away soliciting opinions from old girls under the age of 35 about what we could do ... the format should change from a sit-down lunch to a finger-food buffet; it should be held in the evening rather than at lunchtime; and they should definitely serve more alcohol! The ideas were flowing. But then I stopped to ask myself the question, how would the regular 'old girls' who come year after year feel if we revamped something they knew and loved?

 When making way for the next generation, it is very important to respect the people who are already there.

The next chapter therefore looks at how to bring people together onto the same team and get the best out of these different groups.

 Times change and people change with them, so be aware of the generation you are leading and what motivates them, while being mindful of the longer-serving members too.

U: Uniting Divided People

If you want to make peace with your enemy, you have to work with your enemy. Then he becomes your partner.
– Nelson Mandela

Deep division exists in all walks of life – within families, teams, organizations and countries. Even when you are ultimately part of the same entity, it can be impossible to see 'them' as 'us'. Signs of bitterness and hatred erupt and are very damaging to productivity and well-being. So how can leaders help enemies to make peace with each other and thrive as one?

When have you seen teams, organizations or entities fighting internally to their overall detriment?

Uniting a divided nation

In May 1994, Nelson Mandela became South Africa's first black, democratically elected president. He came to power at a time when the remnants of apartheid where still smouldering, characterized by racial violence and killings.

Imagine being part of a world where racial segregation was the norm – white people were only allowed to marry other whites and public transport, hospitals and living areas were all segregated. For years, a 'them and us' culture was not only actively promoted by government but legally enforced. Whereas laws can be dismantled relatively quickly, years of ingrained thinking can take longer to change. Mandela had a monumental task on his hands to unite a deeply divided nation.

Unite behind a common goal

This visionary leader saw a unique opportunity to unite his deeply divided nation through the 1995 Rugby World Cup, which was to be held in South Africa. He aimed to convince all South African people to unite behind their national team – in other words to believe in a common goal.

The idea to unite people through sport had developed many years before, while Mandela was in prison. Struggling to get on with the guards, Mandela realized that he could use the topic of rugby – a passion of his captors – to strike up a conversation. This enabled the basis of a more positive relationship and was the inspiration for the vision to unite South Africa through sport.

For those of us who enjoy supporting our national team, this may seem pretty easy to achieve, however, sport had become a particularly divisive issue in South Africa. Apartheid had forbidden multiracial teams to play together and, as a result, the national rugby team, the Springboks, had become an acute symbol of racial division within South Africa. The team was generally hated by the non-white population and the thought of getting behind a sport and a team that had alienated them for so long was unimaginable.

Yet magically, on the day of the final between the Springboks and the New Zealand 'All Blacks', South Africans of all races were united in supporting their national team, something that months before had been inconceivable. As Mandela lifted the World Cup, white and black people alike cheered 'Nelson, Nelson, Nelson!' in unanimous support for a once highly controversial leader. So how did he achieve this monumental success in uniting an utterly divided nation?

Influence key people to be your ambassadors

It would have been impossible to unite the country through the Rugby World Cup if the players in the national team had appeared to shun non-white people. Mandela knew the importance of ensuring the team were his ambassadors, therefore he set about developing a personal relationship with them.

Mandela selected his first key ambassador among the players, François Pienaar, the captain of the Springboks, and instigated the beginnings of a personal connection with him. Their acquaintance began with an invitation to meet the president at his office, where Mandela first sowed the seeds of using rugby to unite the nation (it has since culminated in Mandela becoming godfather to one of Pienaar's sons, such is the strength of the bond between these two men).

Mandela also began to develop a relationship with other members of the team. The day before the team's first World Cup match against Australia, Mandela paid a surprise visit to a training session, arriving by helicopter to meet each player personally, expressing his best wishes for their success and to emphasize the opportunity to unite South Africa's people. When leaders go out of their way to meet people and make them feel like they can make a valuable contribution, it can influence them to feel very passionate about fighting for a cause. Mandela's flying visit had this special impact.

The players' determination to contribute to the fight was further cemented midway through the World Cup tournament when the team visited Mandela's former prison on Robben Island – a very moving experience, which brought the enormity of the opportunity home. Mandela had developed a team of ambassadors, demonstrated most poignantly by their commitment to learn the black half of the new South African national anthem, sung in a language different to their native tongue. It is moving to watch footage of Nelson Mandela in his Springbok jersey and cap as the team sing the whole anthem with their hands on their heart. Pienaar was one of just two players not joining in – he has since commented that he was unable to sing as he was choked with emotion.

Type 'Rugby World Cup 1995 South Africa national anthem' into a search engine and watch the team sing on this historic occasion.

Influence both of the conflicting parties to contemplate unity

Party one: Uniting the black population behind the Springboks

Convincing a small team of people to support you is nothing in comparison to the task of convincing large chunks of the population to support something they fundamentally hate, yet Mandela embarked upon making this happen.

South Africa became smothered with the vision slogan 'One team, one country' and the team's only coloured player, Chester Williams, became the face of this marketing plan. However, raising awareness of the vision was not enough, as Mandela found when he attended a rally in KwaZulu-Natal. When he put on a Springbok cap during his speech in support of the national team, he was booed. However, he pacified the crowd with an inspirational retort:

> Amongst you are leaders. Don't be short-sighted. Don't be emotional. Nation-building means that we have to pay a price, in the same way whites have to pay a price. For them to open sports to black people, they are paying a price; for us to say we must now embrace the rugby team is paying a price. That's what we should do.

Support for the Springboks was cemented when the players visited a township the day before their World Cup game with Canada and played with over 300 black children, teaching them how to play rugby. The next day, the township cheered in adoration as South Africa beat Canada 20-0.

In Chapter S: 'Set an example', we talked about the importance of role modelling. It was a powerful gesture of unity for Mandela to wear the Springbok cap and, more importantly, the Springbok jersey on the day of the final (since its green and gold colours were tainted by the association with apartheid). However, over time, people began to follow their leader and wear Springbok memorabilia too.

Party two: Inviting the white population to embrace their whole country's support

Engaging half of a competing body to 'want to play' is pointless if the other party remains hostile. Ultimately, rugby fans would change their behaviour from waving flags that symbolized apartheid to roaring the words 'Nelson, Nelson, Nelson' in adoration for their president.

It would have been easy for Mandela to take away the customs of the white population, such as banning the green and gold jerseys of the Springbok team and getting rid of the national anthem that had existed under apartheid. However, Mandela realized that robbing white South Africans of things that were important to them would make matters worse, not better. He needed to build trust among the white population and this is poignantly demonstrated by the new South African national anthem, which became a hybrid song combining new English lyrics with extracts of the hymn 'Nkosi Sikelel' iAfrika' (the former black anthem 'Lord Bless Africa') and the former national anthem under apartheid, 'Die Stem van Suid-Afrika' ('The Call of South Africa').

THINK ABOUT IT

When you listened to the rugby players singing the new South African national anthem, did you spot the different constituent parts? If you didn't, listen to it again. Reflect on the power of combining these different tunes into one.

A feeling of euphoria swept the *whole* country when the underdog Springbok team won the Rugby World Cup. By the end of the tournament the old flags symbolizing apartheid were gone – the crowd chose to remove them themselves. This shows the power of committing to a desired behaviour (because you want to) rather than simply complying (because you're told you have to).

TRY IT NOW!

If you'd like to learn more about this inspiring and moving story, we highly recommend watching the film *Invictus*, directed by Clint Eastwood, and reading John Carlin's book *Playing the Enemy*, which inspired this film.

IF YOU REMEMBER ONE THING

Focus divided people's attention on something to cheer about rather than fight about. In doing so you'll make 'them' and 'us' into 'we'.

V: Very Stressed!

Nothing gives one person so much advantage over another as to remain always cool and unruffled under all circumstances.
– Thomas Jefferson

A few years ago, my parents took a transatlantic flight that they will never forget. Midway across the Atlantic, their plane hit a patch of extreme turbulence and people were being bounced around the cabin like ping-pong balls, with numerous passengers being sick and others crying and screaming. After recovering from one patch of turbulence the same thing happened again, and again, much to everyone's distress. The incident was so serious that it made the British newspaper headlines the next day, and the pilot later stated that it was the worst turbulence that he had ever encountered.

When my shaken parents called me after the flight, I remember them commenting about the emotional reactions of the crew. Firstly they described their take on the pilot's tannoy announcement. Although the pilot said 'There is nothing to worry about', they could tell from the exceptionally jittery tone of his voice that there clearly *was*. My parents said that the pilot was stuttering to get his words out and that he was reassuring the passengers *so much* that everything would be OK that they seriously questioned whether it would be. To the pilot's credit, he did land the plane safely at its planned destination, for which I owe him my sincere gratitude.

In this extreme situation, the pilot's primary role was to make the correct decisions under pressure, such as 'Do we keep the plane flying at this altitude or attempt to drop below the storm?' Therefore decision making in crisis situations will be explored in the next chapter. However, since the ability to make decisions can be vastly *impaired* if you can't keep control of your emotions, this chapter looks at ways to keep calm under pressure.

THINK ABOUT IT Think about situations where you have been led by others in high-pressure situations. What impact did their emotions have on you?

Returning to our transatlantic flight, my parents also relayed a rumour concerning the behaviour of an air stewardess working in another part of the cabin. Reportedly passengers heard her say three times, 'We are going to crash.' It has since been disputed as to whether this was true or not; however, you can imagine the massively negative impact that this would have had, if indeed it did occur. If the crew comes across as scared, and they have been on many hundreds more flights than you, then you know that something is seriously wrong. And my parents said that it was certainly

174

true that the crew looked and sounded very rattled by the situation. It is interesting to ask yourself what impact that pilot's tannoy announcement also had on the crew.

Imagine that you were a member of crew on board that flight. With your own life at risk too, how easy would it be to maintain your composure under extreme pressure?

How good are you naturally at maintaining emotional composure under pressure?

How do you stay calm under extreme pressure?

Given the importance of the leadership team staying calm under pressure, the key question that follows is: how do you do it? Let's take a look at some of the ways to keep calm and carry on.

1. Recruit people who can handle pressure

While many of us would find it very hard to maintain composure in a life-or-death situation, it is fair to say that some people naturally handle pressure much better than others. So before accepting a high-pressured leadership position, it is worth asking yourself, 'How well do I handle stress?'

Whether you look at a renowned world leader such as Sir Winston Churchill (who led Britain to victory in World War II) or the leader of my teenage Guide troop (who found herself stuck in monsoon camping conditions with muddy, damp and extremely unhappy children), stress is something that comes with the job. If you are considering taking a leadership position, or recruiting someone else for one, you need to be aware that stress is almost certain to come with the territory.

You can think of stress as a bucket of water. Once the bucket is full, it only takes a single drop, something minor, to tip a person over the edge and visibly display stress. But key to the issue is that some people will have naturally smaller metaphorical buckets than others, so it doesn't take much before their bucket is overflowing.

Before putting yourself (or appointing others) to a stressful leadership role, ask, 'Is this for me?' A clever recruitment campaign by the British Royal Marines depicted extremely tough and stressful working conditions, ending with the caption '99.99% need not apply'. It is important to give yourself (or others) a realistic preview of the stress levels that a role will actually entail and to be confident that the bucket is large enough to handle the demands of the role.

In the following chapter we'll explore the Apollo 13 crisis, where a serious explosion happened on board the spaceship as it journeyed towards the moon. When you listen to the recordings of the real-life incident, it is eerie how calm the astronauts' communications are in the face of death. In a documentary about the incident, Flight Director Gene Kranz commented that, prior to working for NASA, both he and the crew had been fighter-jet pilots and were used to facing danger on a daily basis. Part of NASA's recruitment criteria had been to appoint people who could stay calm under pressure, and that attitude was critical in a crisis.

2. Find an outlet for stress

Both work and life will add to the level of stress in our buckets. So leaders need to find a way to lower the water level. If they don't, and something stressful happens during the course of a day's work, they risk 'losing it' in front of their people. This can have very negative consequences, particularly in high-pressured situations when people look to the leader to instil calm in themselves.

Sometimes people need an emotional outlet, such as a person to let off steam to. In this instance, leaders need to be very aware of who they choose to display their stress to. For example, in a high-panic situation on board a struggling aircraft, ask yourself, who is/are the best person/people for a flight attendant to communicate fears to? The passengers, or other members of the crew? Sometimes you cannot control how you feel, but leaders need to control *who* they choose to display these feelings to.

Another outlet for stress can be something practical such as exercising. It is always important to make time for stress-relieving activities, being mindful that they are usually the first things that go out of the window when under pressure and yet they are the most needed. Despite this good advice, even with good intentions, it isn't always possible to pop out for a lunchtime run in the middle of a crisis, so you need to find another way to quickly relieve tension.

Interestingly my parents commented that during their plane journey from hell, at an appropriate moment the flight attendants served up impromptu gin and tonics. This created humour and passengers and staff alike were distracted from focusing on the situation by instead concentrating on not spilling a drop of this precious beverage. When using humour in a stressful situation, the word 'appropriate' is key, but remember it can be a powerful tool to alleviate stress.

What are the most effective ways you have found to release stress in an appropriate fashion?

Who is a key confidant(e) that you can rely on to voice your concerns to in a safe environment?

---

3. Be outcome-focused

Life will continually throw us unexpected stressful curveballs, as I found when I recently took a clean cup out of the kitchen cupboard at a company I was working for. As I pulled the cup out from the overhead cupboard, much to my horror, I was showered from head to toe in cold tea. For some bizarre reason, someone had put their used cup back in the cupboard and I was literally wearing the consequences of that careless act.

When things like this happen, our typical (and wholly justifiable) reaction is to get angry: 'How could someone be so stupid and inconsiderate? I'm soaking wet, how will I continue my work without changing? Have you seen the state of me? My new outfit is totally ruined. I'm really embarrassed', etc. We *react*.

In this instance, I was standing in front of two trainees who were attending the leadership training session that I was running that day, ironically focusing on behaviour under pressure! One of them turned to me and asked how I managed to stay so calm.

During the next section of the course, right on cue with the slides I had already prepared, I explained the psychological principle of **ERO**, which stands for **Event, Response, Outcome**.

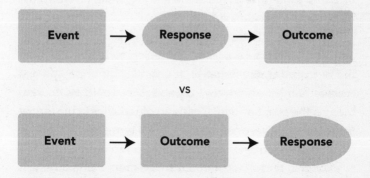

In life, *events* happen to which we typically *react* and get an *outcome*. The outcome of me flipping out in the office kitchen would probably have been to create a poor impression in front of my trainees, and, crucially, would not have altered the fact that I was covered in tea.

Instead, when something stressful happens, you need to be outcome-focused and think, 'What do I want the outcome to be?' Crucially you then choose the most appropriate response to achieve that outcome. It may still be the outcome you would have displayed by simply reacting, but the difference is you have *consciously* chosen this based on the outcome you want.

After the tea incident, I wanted to continue with where I was previously headed, making a cup of tea and getting on with my course. So instead of focusing my energy on getting angry, I focused on working out how I needed to respond in order to achieve this – I took up my course participants' kind offer to make me a drink, while I went to the bathroom to get cleaned up.

Linking back to the example of a panicking air stewardess (*reacting*) in the face of life-threatening turbulence (*event*), the *outcome* is very negative. It unsettles other people and makes them question how capable she would be to lead them in the event an actual crisis unfolded. Plus in the longer term, this has a very negative impact in terms of the damage done to her reputation and that of her employer.

For this reason, at moments of extreme pressure, it is critical that leaders think about the outcome they want – ideally the air stewardess should have reassured her passengers through her actions, and, if this wasn't possible, she should certainly have removed herself from the visibility of the passengers to ensure that she did not create a highly undesirable action.

Being realistic, it is difficult to control your reactions under extreme pressure; however, over time, if you can learn to handle the little things in life, such as getting covered in cups of tea, you can get into the habit of being outcome-focused in the most severe situations. This is a powerful mindset that can help you in any stressful situation in life.

When have you naturally been outcome-focused under pressure and chosen your response to get the best possible outcome? When have you reacted to a negative event and with hindsight wish you had chosen your response more carefully?

Next time you find yourself in a stressful situation, be outcome-focused and choose your response.

Leaders need to be like a swan – even if you are paddling frantically underneath you need to be seen to be composed, otherwise you risk instilling panic in others.

(And beware of seemingly clean cups in kitchen cupboards!)

W: Wrong Direction, Right Decisions

The work in this room is final. The decisions are final.
The team in this room must be prepared not only to
make the decisions but to live with the results that occur.
– Gene Kranz

On 13 April 1970, the crew of the Apollo 13 spaceflight originally destined to land on the moon carried out a routine procedure to stir the oxygen tanks on board the craft. As they flicked the switch, the crew heard and felt a large explosion and calmly uttered the immortal words, 'Houston, we've had a problem.'

It became increasingly apparent that the mission to the moon was over and, with a very badly damaged spacecraft, the lives of the astronauts hung perilously in the balance.

Flight Director Gene Kranz quickly recognized that the Mission Control team had to go into rescue mode, meaning that they had to not only make decisions but to make them fast. So what enabled the crew of a crippled ship to even have a chance at survival? Let's take a look at the factors that supported the sound and timely decision-making Gene Kranz and the team demonstrated under such immense pressure.

1. Contingency planning and simulation training
In a high-pressured situation, wherever possible, people need to instinctively know how to react, which means

having had contingency plans worked out in advance and training so that the team is proficient beforehand.

Simulation training can be very useful for a number of reasons. It gives a realistic preview of what *can* happen; it drills into people *what to do*, so that everyone knows exactly how to react and how others will react; it can save precious time in situations that require swift action, because people already know what to do.

For the crew of Apollo 13 simulation training was life saving. As oxygen levels fell rapidly in the ship's living quarters (the Command Module) the crew actioned a contingency plan that they had practised but never expected to use. They were forced to rapidly evacuate to the Lunar Module, the vehicle that was intended to land on the moon, before oxygen supplies in the Command Module ran out. The crew successfully achieved the transfer with only moments to spare.

Moving briefly from space to the rugby pitch, Sir Clive Woodward, who led his rugby team and country to World Cup-winning success in 2003, is also a firm believer in the importance of contingency planning. So much so that he said he spent more time with the England rugby team training *inside the classroom* than *outside* on the pitch!

In that classroom, the team tried to think through all of the different scenarios that they could face during their games. It meant that when things did go wrong, the players didn't panic and helplessly wonder what to do next, they just got on and executed the plan they had previously agreed, and clearly it was a successful strategy.

Obviously life isn't as simple as a rugby match – it is harder to plan for every eventuality. But even the act of working through a small sub-set of possible scenarios can increase knowledge and confidence and help people to make timely and accurate decisions under pressure.

2. Risk assess

Flight Director Gene Kranz had a fundamental decision to make – how to get the crew back to earth? Option one was a direct abort. They would turn the ship around and head straight back to earth in a day and a half. The problem with this was that it would require use of the spaceship's engine, which could have been damaged in the explosion, and there was concern that the damaged engine could blow up.

The second option was to slingshot around the moon and return back to Earth, which would take four to five days. The problem with that approach was that the Lunar Module was designed for just two men for only two days, which would put a strain on how long the power and oxygen would last.

Kranz decided that he did not wish to take the risk of the first option (aborting) and instead made the decision to slingshot around the moon and trust his team to find the answers to any issues that would arise from choosing this scenario. Looking at this in terms of risk assessment, Kranz made the decision that the *impact* of failure from both options was severe (i.e. death) but the *probability* of failure was higher for the abort option, so Kranz abandoned that idea.

When making difficult decisions, leaders need to evaluate options in terms of both severity and probability:

Severity	Probability
Low impact	Low probability
Medium impact	Medium probability
High impact	High probability
Catastrophic impact	Certain to occur

They can also take into account the pros and cons of various solutions; for example, the slingshot option bought the Apollo crew extra time to work out solutions, which would not have been available in the attempt of a direct abort.

3. Know your environment

Leaders need to have a good awareness of their environment, proactively looking for issues so that they can act quickly should they occur. A leader of a major event control room commented that when an event is running smoothly, he doesn't sit drinking coffee and having a chat, he's constantly scanning the CCTV monitors to keep abreast of what is happening and proactively be on the lookout for the first signs of trouble.

Back at Mission Control, constant monitoring of the environment was also a priority and therefore the team quickly detected another potential crisis. The carbon dioxide levels in the Lunar Module began to rise dangerously high – the Lunar Module had only been designed to hold two people (on their journey to the moon's surface), but, once it became a lifeboat, it held three people, all exhaling carbon dioxide.

Proactive monitoring of the environment bought the team time – the astronauts couldn't have seen toxic carbon dioxide concentrations, so without Mission Control's awareness of the situation on board the craft the situation could quickly have turned fatal.

Fortunately there were spare carbon dioxide filters available in the Command Module; however, a design inconsistency meant that the Command Module filters were square-shaped, while the Lunar Module filters were round. This meant that the astronauts would have to create an adaptor, which would literally enable a square peg to fit in a round hole. Fortunately the Mission Control team knew exactly what items were available on the ship. In a race against time, they prototyped a solution, using only the objects that the crew would have to hand, from duct tape to plastic from their underwear.

In difficult situations the proposed solution is often to throw more resources at the problem – more money, more time or more people. As a leader, you need to be aware of resource limitations and not try to solve problems with resources that you don't have. Sometimes there are simply no more resources to go around. In which case your challenge is to use what you *do* have very wisely.

4. Ensure decisions are executed as you intended

The best decision, poorly executed, can end in disaster. It was one thing for the Mission Control to come up with an adaptor for the air filter; executing that solution was another matter. The Mission Control team had to carefully communicate the proposed course of action to those who would implement it, with no room for error. Communicating decisions becomes even more difficult in the face of pressure.

 For this activity you need two people who each have a photograph of their own house and pens and paper.

- Step one: ask the people to sit back-to-back and ask one person to describe their house, while the other sits in silence and draws it.

- In step two, reverse the roles and repeat the exercise, but this time the individual drawing the picture is allowed to ask questions.

- What is the difference in outcome between the two drawings?

Leaders need to understand the difference between passive listening and active describing. Telling people what decisions have been made, why they were made and what needs to be done is important. But you may also need to check understanding of the message to ensure that any required action is executed as intended. One of the best ways to ensure this is to ask the person receiving the instructions to relay them back to the person giving them. In doing so, the recipient has to actively utilize their memory and recall the instructions, while the relaying of what they're doing helps them prepare by actually walking through what needs to be done.

Fortunately the crew of the Apollo 13 spaceship did accurately hear the instructions communicated to them and the carbon dioxide crisis was averted.

- What contingency plans would it be prudent for you to make in your role as a leader?

- What knowledge gaps do you currently have about your leadership environment that would be prudent to fill?

- When communicating decisions, what can you do to ensure that they have been correctly implemented?

We also suggest that you rent a copy of the fantastic movie *Apollo 13*. As you watch it, make a list of qualities that make character Gene Kranz an outstanding leader. In case you don't know the ending, we won't spoil the outcome!

Following the mission, Gene Kranz was awarded the Presidential Medal of Freedom. He was a determined leader who refused to believe that failure was an option and inspired everyone to perform at their very best under the most extreme conditions imaginable.

 In the darkest of hours, leaders need to display a compelling determination to succeed, focusing on making the best possible decisions in high-pressured situations.

X: eXit

There's a trick to the graceful exit. It begins with the vision to recognize when a job, a life stage, a relationship is over – and to let go. It means leaving what's over without denying its validity of its past importance in our lives.
– Ellen Goodman

Over time we've come to realize that the best time to leave a party is when you are still having a great time. Inevitably, the party will finish, and yes, if you leave early you *might* miss the most brilliant experience imaginable. But chances are that things will start to get a bit messy and, with aching feet from those gorgeous but horribly uncomfortable new heels, or the beginnings of a hangover, you'll reach a point where you realized you stayed too long. In contrast, when you leave on a high, you can look back fondly and people will remember you with a smile on your face. You'll also be better placed to get up and take on the next day.

You may have heard the saying that 'all good things come to an end', and the same is true for leadership. Just as leaders need to be self-aware in their rise to and tenure in a position of power, they also need to be self-aware about their timing and manner of exit. Failure to do so can lead to an unfortunate stain on your reputation and a sense of bitterness that may never leave you or the people you led.

A leadership lifecycle

You can think of leadership as having three distinct stages:

- Entry: a period with a high degree of uncertainty as the fledgling leader struggles to deal with the responsibilities of their new position, the aftermath of the previous leader and to develop future strategy.

- Consolidation: the period where the leader's work begins to produce results, building a solid base for the organization's future.

- Decline: the point where the leader's performance begins to deteriorate. They can be perceived as tired and lacking in focus, stuck in their ways. People may begin to gossip about their capability, triggering a (perhaps justified) sense of paranoia about their ability to hold onto their position.

Leaders who spend too long in the 'decline' stage can become real threats to organizations and teams that they have led successfully for many years. Therefore strong leaders need to minimize the amount of time spent in this phase, quitting ahead of serious decline, leaving behind a fruitful legacy and gracefully transitioning into the next phase of their lives.

THINK ABOUT IT

Think of examples of leaders, famous or personal acquaintances, who have failed to leave gracefully *and* others who stepped down just at the right time.

What impact did the timing of their departure have on themselves and others?

The fall of Margaret Thatcher

In a BBC documentary about former British Prime Minister Margaret Thatcher, ex-colleagues comment that, with hindsight, she should have left office after a landmark ten years in office. Despite already facing tensions within her party regarding her leadership, at this point she could have resigned gracefully – still tasting the sweetness of her ten-year anniversary cake and hearing applause ringing in her ears.

However, history would reveal that things would not end so positively. Linking back to the leadership cycle previously described, she had hoped to stay in the 'consolidation' phase for longer than she ultimately did.

Margaret Thatcher *had* planned her exit from office. In her mind, she wanted to go on to fight and win a fourth election and then hand over to a worthy successor a couple of years later. This would give her time to complete unfinished business and groom a successor to be ready to take on her precious work. But she admitted herself that the best-laid plans sometimes fail.

When it comes to the timing and method of exit, leaders need to be astute enough to know when to 'call it a day', so that they don't spend too much time in the 'decline' phase, to the detriment of themselves and their people. Thatcher increasingly experienced a division between herself and senior government figures, reportedly leading to hostile ultimatums from them, such as 'Do this or I will resign.' Support wavered as members of her party began to question not only 'Can our party win the next election if she is the leader?', but more personally, 'Will anyone vote for me if she stays – will I be able to retain my own parliamentary seat?' Eventually a leadership challenge forced her departure, at the point where she realized she no longer had the support of her party, including her closest allies. It was a sad end to a memorable period of leadership.

The departure of Bill Gates

Contrast the awkward end of Thatcher's reign with the standing ovation received by Bill Gates on his last day as a Microsoft employee in June 2008. Since Gates co-founded the organization, it was literally 'his baby' and the tears in his eyes on his last day reflect how hard it must have been to let go.

Bill Gates slowly weaned himself off Microsoft, firstly stepping down from CEO to chief software architect in 2000. Then, in 2006, he began to reduce the number of hours that he worked, until eventually ending his time as a Microsoft employee in 2008.

This graceful departure from full-time employment has enabled Bill Gates to remain as chairman of Microsoft to this day. Rather than being an unwanted leader, Gates can still provide advice to 'his baby' on important issues, while devoting the majority of his time and energy to his philanthropic organization – the Bill & Melinda Gates Foundation, established in 2000.

The Bill & Melinda Gates Foundation has been key to Bill Gates' successful departure from Microsoft, as it gave him a new focus. In a newspaper interview with the *Seattle Post-Intelligencer*, he stated, 'I'm not a sit-on-the-beach type.' Instead he redirects the time and energy previously spent at Microsoft to his foundation, providing an alternative source of purpose and power, making it easier to wean himself from day-to-day life at Microsoft. After all, they say the best way to get over an old relationship is to find a new one! Even when you've held a fantastic position, there is always another exciting door to open, you just have to find it.

Seek PERMA not POWER

PERMA is a model developed by Martin Seligman, founder of the Positive Psychology movement, which seeks to understand what makes a person flourish in life. PERMA stands for:

P – positive emotions (i.e. feeling happy on a day-to-day basis)

E – engagement (being positively absorbed in activities you undertake)
R – relationships (positive relationships with other people)
M – meaning (feeling a sense of purpose)
A – achievement (feeling the sense of accomplishment).

Seligman hypothesizes that if these five areas are satisfied, a person will experience a feeling of well-being. In other words, if you find your day pleasant, you are interested in what you are doing, you interact positively with others, feel that your time is spent meaningfully and you achieve a valued output for your time, you will feel satisfied.

During Thatcher's period of 'decline', how well do you think her PERMA criteria would have been satisfied?

During the course of Bill Gates' philanthropic work, how well do you think his PERMA criteria are satisfied?

Although a leadership role may feel like the be-all and end-all, remember that there are other ways to find satisfaction with life. The longer you hold onto a declining position of power, the more your PERMA criteria are likely to suffer.

Bill Gates benefitted from building his new focus well before he divorced himself from his old focus. Just as it is important to invest in self-development time for a future role, it is also important to make time to consider 'What next?' after this leadership role.

THINK ABOUT IT

In future, what can you do that will:

- Be enjoyable on a day-to-day basis?
- Keep your attention absorbed?

- Enable you to maximize the benefits of relationships with others?

- Give you a satisfying sense of purpose?

- Enable you to feel like you are achieving something?

IF YOU REMEMBER ONE THING

It is prudent to ask yourself, 'When is it the right time to leave this party and what do I want to do tomorrow?'

Y: Your Successor

The function of leadership is to produce more leaders,
not more followers.
– Ralph Nader

Every leader will one day have to hand over the reigns to another. The impact of having a leadership change, especially a senior one, can be massive. A change in leader, if handled badly, can be disruptive, threatening not just what has been achieved, but its very future.

Take, for example, the case of Margaret Thatcher who we looked at in the previous chapter. Although Thatcher had set off with good intentions to groom a successor, when Thatcher *actually* departed office, forced out due to her increasing unpopularity, she left behind a bitterly divided political party – fighting among itself, while the 'contenders for the throne' jostled for position against their rivals. The way these events happened have left a scar on her party that to this day, over twenty years on, has not completely healed.

THINK ABOUT IT If, due to some change in your circumstances, you were no longer able to carry out your leadership duties, what would happen a) to the achievement of your vision, and b) to those who you lead?

Having a succession plan is part of your success

A highly successful managing director of a prestigious global company once said to us that one of the key roles of a leader is to replace themselves in their role.

He went on to explain that no leader could move on to the next challenge in their life unless they had invested in growing those who would take over. If a leader couldn't move on when the time had come because there was no capable replacement, the leader had failed in this key part of their job.

Having put all your time and energy into an organization or initiative, you should aim to leave it in the best possible hands. You therefore need to groom the next generation of leaders who can take your vision forward and enhance it over time. You don't want to leave a moving car without a competent driver at the wheel.

The time to do this is now

When should you start to focus on replacing yourself? The answer is: as soon as possible. As a leader, your time at the helm may be limited by statute (i.e. a president for four years), by a change in your popularity, health issues, or in some very unfortunate cases by a disaster. Some of these can be foreseen and addressed, others can't. Therefore, the sooner you can focus on committing your organizational resources to identifying, retaining and developing the talent to lead in the future, the better.

The more embedded you are within your organization the more difficult it may feel to want to commit to finding your successor. Take the case of billionaire businessman Warren Buffet, the 'Sage of Omaha' as he is known affectionately, who has proven to be one of the leading investors in history. Now in his 80s, he has yet to step aside as the CEO of Berkshire Hathaway, the investment and insurance company that he has passionately built up. He even kept going after a diagnosis of prostate cancer in 2012.

Remember that as a leader you have a responsibility to those that you lead and those that have bought into your vision. Without a successor in place, you are asking all of the parties that bought into and backed your vision to accept an ongoing risk that it will fail if something happens. Warren finally acknowledged that when he wrote to shareholders of Berkshire Hathaway in 2012 and stated that he had found not only the person who would replace him, but also two further candidates as back-up.

Who should identify the successor?

Leaders aren't carbon copies. Even somebody with Warren's experience and success couldn't create a replica to take over when the time is right for him to step aside. And why would he want to? His way of investing in the past may not be successful in future times. New leaders need to adapt to new challenges, not keep conquering old ones.

The people involved in selecting the successor should be wider than just the leader that they are replacing, so that an objective assessment can be made. This means involving (where applicable) the board (who have responsibility for the ongoing running of the organization), human resources (who can measure the suitability of candidates), other senior leaders and managers within the organization, plus key stakeholders or shareholders.

Together they can best identify the capabilities and skills needed from this new leader given the challenges they will face in the role. Also, when each of these parties reaches agreement, they reinforce their commitment to the vision and their buy-in to the new leader.

Better the devil you know

Ideally a leadership successor should be drawn from the pool of talent that exists within your organization. This pool of people is already familiar with its vision, its mission statement, the operations of the business and vitally those who it serves.

The value of this experience was revealed in 2008 at the company Starbucks, when its founder, Howard Schultz, had to return to the helm after eight years. Schultz admits that he had not spent much time considering a succession plan when it was completely his responsibility to do so. So, with Starbucks undergoing serious challenges to its business under the leadership of Jim Donald, Schultz retook the CEO role in 2008.

The reason Schultz felt he had to do this was due to the company not being managed according to its established values. Because Schultz had grown up within the business, knowing its operations intricately, he believed that when it came to making tough decisions, he was better positioned to be the leader during a time of crisis for the company.

 Draw up a list of internal succession candidates. Once you have this list, consider the following questions:

- How well do they command the respect of the people they work with?

- How well do they command the respect of the clients they work for?

- How well do they command the respect of those who give us backing?

- How well do their actions represent the organization's guiding values?

- What are their core skills and strengths?

- What ambitions do they have for themselves?

- What ambitions do they have for the organization and the vision?

When you begin to consider potential successors along these lines you should start to be able to objectively separate candidates out. If you find that you are not able to answer these questions sufficiently, or feel that you have some blind spots with some candidates, this highlights that you need to further engage with each candidate and those around them to obtain insightful feedback about them.

Of course it may not always be possible to grow the leader from within the organization if there is a lack of potential or resources to do so. In which case attention will focus on outside possibilities. If this happens, a succession plan considered in plenty of time will allow the external candidate time to join the organization and immerse themselves within it before they attain the leadership role.

An external candidate could also have experience of your organization even without working within it, for example through being a key partner, a shareholder or a client. This will enable them to appreciate what is unique and exemplary about your people, its culture and its vision, while also spotting greater strategic potential opportunities on top of what you're currently doing.

The best interview is to let them do the job

One of the most interesting things about the TV show *The Apprentice* is to see how people from different walks of life do at the challenges that they are set. Week after week they are assigned a different task to see how they perform. The results we see are borne from (among other things) their values, attitude to teamwork, social interactions and ambition. We see how they behave as they carry out other people's orders and how they behave when they are the ones whose turn it is to lead.

Now, we are not suggesting you set up your own edition of *The Apprentice* in your organization (although you can if you want to!). What we are saying is that there is no better way to see how a person performs as a leader than by actually getting them to demonstrate it. The closer the scenario is to what they face in real life the better, as the behaviours and results you'll see will be a closer approximation.

To enable other leaders to develop, the incumbent leader must be able to let them grow into the role. When Steve Jobs required medical leave from Apple in 2004 and 2009, Tim Cook, Apple's executive vice-president of worldwide sales and operations and later the chief operating officer, took over the controls. Steve was still involved in the strategic decisions, but Tim's profile and responsibilities were growing. Then, in 2011, when Steve could no longer carry out his duties as CEO of Apple, in his resignation letter to the board he recommended implementing the longstanding succession plan and install Tim as permanent CEO. When Tim took over on a full-time basis he therefore did not come as a surprise. Apple's customers and employees knew him and, vitally, those who invest in Apple's vision had already seen what he could do.

TRY IT NOW! Write out a leadership description for your role. Consider some of the following questions:

- What are the key demands that you are faced with?

- Who are some of the key stakeholders that you have to report to?

- What strategic decisions will you soon have to take?

- What issues require solutions to them?

Use this leadership description to demonstrate to potential successors the task that they need to take on. Where possible, start letting them experience increased responsibility in delivering on some of these. Remember that the leader needs to stand aside and let their successors grow, so be prepared to let them work out the 'how' in how they overcome obstacles and create solutions. Offer guidance if it is asked for and do not take the reins over from them unless there is a serious risk to which the organization would be exposed.

IF YOU REMEMBER ONE THING A leader's time comes and goes – when it's time to go, the leader needs to have put in place and developed the leaders who can continue the vision and the mission according to the values and culture in place.

Z: Zeal

*The most powerful weapon on earth is
the human soul on fire.*
– Field Marshal Ferdinand Foch

Artists know that white is a very special colour. Although on its own, a white tube of paint used on a white canvas would be pretty useless, when mixed with other pigments it becomes a very valuable asset. White works with every other colour to create the perfect shade.

At the start of this book, we described leadership as an artist's palette, where the colours represent the strengths that support leaders to excel. Now imagine that an artist's tube of white paint represents zeal – a sense of passion, fervour and enthusiasm, leading to the exertion of significant effort. Although an abundance of energy *alone* achieves nothing, when combined with other leadership activities, it becomes a magic ingredient that creates the perfect outcome.

*Passion is, and will always be, a necessary ingredient.
Even the world's best business plan won't produce any
return if it is not backed with passion.*
– Howard Schultz

We've covered leaders from many walks of life in this book. If you could have any one of them (or any that we haven't mentioned) be your mentor for the day, who would it be?

Once you told them your vision, imagine that they brought their own knowledge, skills and zeal to help you achieve that. How much would that energize you to just go for it?

Let's paint our final picture of successful leadership from the A–Z of this book, underpinned by a hint of our metaphorical white paint, zeal.

A. **Aspiration:** Have passionate desire to achieve a future goal.

B. **Backing:** When you have total belief in your vision, remain determined to secure the backing required to bring it to life, no matter how many knock-backs you encounter.

C. **Compelling communication:** Spread the vision with infectious enthusiasm. Help others to understand where you are now and where you need to get to, creating an enticing sense of urgency and excitement about the prospect of achieving it.

D. **Decide your strategy:** In order to achieve your vision you will need to decide your strategy, ensuring you survive in the short term, focusing on your core strengths and using them to overcome the barriers that will hold you back.

E. **Execute:** In order to execute your strategy you need the right personnel in place and to break the overall goal down into the right sequence of smaller activities. As the leader you need to monitor your team's progression and set and monitor the standard.

F. **Form the team:** TEAM – 'Together Everyone Achieves More'. Enthusiastically build and grow your team, encouraging members to get to know each other personally and professionally and to feel inspired to work together to achieve a common goal.

G. **Guiding values:** Used well, values infect the culture of an organization, positively impacting everyday decisions and actions. Leaders should display a passion for the values of the organization, proactively bringing them to life through their language and actions.

H. **Help underperformers:** Leaders are like watering cans – given the right care and conditions, even the weakest seedlings can thrive. It takes time and energy to support struggling individuals, but persevere and you'll be amazed at how much they can grow.

I. **Inspire top performance:** Little things can make a big difference – strive to learn everyone's names, channel your energy towards praising individual efforts/performance and demonstrate that you care. Great leaders make everyone feel important.

J. **Joyful working:** There is a scientifically proven link between a positive mood and improved creativity and performance. Aim to infect your workplace with a positive, energized spirit and remember that work and play don't have to be polar opposites.

K. **Keep stakeholders onside:** Form and maintain relationships with your key stakeholders, particularly the high-importance ones. Demonstrate a keen interest to meet their needs and actively welcome their input on matters that affect them.

L. **Listen:** Demonstrate a passion for your people – aim to meet their needs and resolve their issues by wearing a 'listening HAT' – *Hear* their concerns, *Act* upon them and *Tell* people what you have done.

M. **Motivate:** Be eager to understand what motivates your people – keep them motivated and they will keep trying their best for you.

N. **No more negativity:** To raise low morale, you have to first look to your own mood – demotivated leaders will struggle to motivate others. Then aim to create a spirit of camaraderie, being seen to take your share of the pain, and launch into battle against a common enemy.

O. **Outside your comfort zone:** Leaders can be like magnets, attracting people to leave their comfort zones. Infect others with enthusiasm to leave their comfort zone through changing the association with leaving it from bad (e.g. risky, stressful) to good (e.g. exciting, rewarding).

P. **Progress change:** Persevere in leading your people through the stages of change – pre-contemplation, contemplation, action, maintenance and termination.

Q. **Qualities of leaders:** If you want to be the best leader possible, focus your attention on understanding what aspects of your personality help you and which aspects hinder your performance. Make a concerted effort to consciously modify the more negative aspects of your behaviour.

R. **Respect and integrity:** Work hard to maintain your integrity – once lost, it is hard to retrieve, and difficult to succeed as a leader.

S. **Set an example:** Be the change you want to see in the world – if you want to see certain desirable behaviour, or eliminate bad practice, focus your efforts on being a positive role model.

T. **Times change:** There is a saying that change is the only constant. As technology changes and new generations enter the workforce, leaders need to inspire change to meet new needs and challenges, while concurrently supporting longer-standing members to feel welcomed, valued and comfortable.

U. **Unite divided people:** Demonstrate strong willpower to unite even the most divided of people behind a common goal. Influence people to see that having something to celebrate together is far better than bitterness and hatred.

V. **Very stressed!:** Keep control of your energy – channel stress to create focused determination – don't just react, know what outcome you want and choose your response.

W. **Wrong direction, right decision:** In the darkest of hours, leaders need to display a compelling determination to succeed, focusing on making the best possible decisions in high-pressure situations.

X. **eXit:** Leaders who have overstayed their welcome create toxic energy around them. Just as you need to be enthusiastic about starting your leadership term on a high, you also need to be focused to ensure that it ends on a high, leaving a positive legacy behind you.

Y. **Your successor:** If you want the fruits of your labour to be sustained well beyond your tenure, you need to devote energy to selecting and developing your successor well in advance of your intended departure.

Z. **Zeal:** Finally, when, after painstaking effort, you write the last word in a story, reflect on the passion you felt for your project, the determination you exhibited through tough times and take pride in the dedication to your cause.

Acknowledgements

With thanks to:

- Carlo DiClemente for permission to detail the Stages of Change model

- Jack Zenger and Joseph Folkman for permission to detail their Leadership Tent model

- Martin Seligman for permission to detail his PERMA model.

Index